THE BOOK LIFE

*Life's Pathway to Peace through
the True and Living God*

VICTOR BRADFORD

Order this book online at www.trafford.com
or email orders@trafford.com

Most Trafford titles are also available at major online book retailers.

Print information available on the last page.

ISBN: 978-1-4269-3114-7 (sc)
ISBN: 978-1-4269-3115-4 (hc)

Library of Congress Control Number: 2010905017

Trafford rev. 04/22/2015

www.trafford.com
North America & international
toll-free: 1 888 232 4444 (USA & Canada)
fax: 812 355 4082

Author's Introduction

This book was written to encourage men, women and especially children (because they are tomorrow's future) of all walks of life to live a life filled with joy, happiness and peace. Moreover, to show how life itself can bring much sadness, low self-esteem of one's self, depression, and last but not least, a desire to just give up living the life that God has set forth for us to live.

My desire is also to reveal in the hearts of many around the world how beautiful life can be when living to please God and how miserable life can be when living to please one's self.

This book contains written information to show the many trials, tribulations of this world, due to the evil that is in the hearts of many around the world as I have seen it through my eyes over the years I have been upon this earth. A testimony of my life was also written through the pages of this book, to give further encouragement to those that have experienced similar situations in their lives.

May God open the hearts and eyes of everyone who read this book that they may receive every word with gladness, and also bring understanding of life itself, and to give guidance and direction in the life that God has so freely given to us all.

(No names will be revealed for anonymity purposes)

CHAPTER ONE

The Beginning

My life began in a city called Washington, DC. As long as I have been upon this earth, I have never seen my real mother and father which has always been a very hurtful feeling that I have endured for many years.

I can only remember back to when I was five years old. What happened before then I do not know. My foster family informed me that I had been in an orphanage for my first five years. The name of the orphanage was called Junior Village. I would have loved to find out what I endured while I was there. As far as I know Junior Village is no longer operating or in service.

I will share how my early life developed when I was with my foster parents. Since I was never adopted, I never shared their last name. I had two older foster brothers (ages 11 and 12) and one foster sister (age 13) who was the oldest sibling in the family.

I was the youngest in the family (age 5) and in the beginning things were going well. I seemed to have bonded somewhat with my older brother. He seemed to give me more attention than to the others.

As far as I can remember during my first year in my foster home, I had a lot of fun such as snowball fights, getting toys to play with, and looking at fun shows and sporting events on the television.

At that time life was really good to me. However, I often found myself thinking about where and who my real mother and father were. I never had the nerve to ask my foster parents that question because they may have felt that I was not happy being with them.

I remember starting elementary school at Bunker Hill Elementary located in northeast Washington, D.C. It was in a nice middle-class neighborhood just like in my foster home area.

At that time I was meeting other kids in the area where I lived. Now at this point and time of my life even though I felt blessed, life itself was beginning to reveal to me the unpleasant things in life such as being teased by other kids in school, about my having a big nose, and about how my clothes looked. I must confess that those kids truly hurt my feelings almost every day of my life. The sad part about it is I never talked to anyone about it. Moreover, by me never saying anything, some of the kids began to pick on me – like push me around. I was told that I was really timid and from the look of things I guess I was.

Now about the kids in my immediate neighborhood: From the day after one of my brothers told the kids in the area that I was an orphan, I was teased day in and day out. The way they said 'orphan' I felt that I was nothing but a piece of trash. Yes, at that point in time of my existence, life was revealing to me the cruelty that is in the hearts of us all. I was feeling really down and experiencing very low self-esteem.

This torture continued for the next two years. Life had more cruelty in store for me. In my foster home things were beginning to take a turn for the worst. For instance, when my foster mother and father would go out to dinner or to some special engagement, my foster brothers and sister would take me down to the basement and take turns beating on me with their hands and elbows. They made sure to never left marks on me because they knew where to hit me and make it hurt severely and would dare me not to tell. To this day I have no idea why they did this to me. The only thing I can think of is that my foster mother took me everywhere with her. She showed me so much love and maybe they were just jealous. During all of this traumatic drama that I was enduring I managed to continue to go to school and do my best to get a proper education. Life did show me the importance of an education. Without a proper education it would be very hard to get ahead in life such as getting a good job, knowing how to count money and especially knowing how to talk to people in a proper way. School has always been fun to me in spite of what I was going through. I did manage to meet other kids I could get along with. During the years in elementary school I had come to learn that I was slow mentally. I did not allow it to get me down. Just as long as I was able to continue to play sports, I was happy.

CHAPTER TWO

Now, about my being mentally slow: I learned that by me not being able to remember what I read without reading it to or three times, my speech was somewhat impaired. Just having a hard time understanding a lot of things labeled me as being slow. I often think about the things I went through that could have contributed to my being slow, if not contributed to but may have had a strong effect – such as being poisoned by my foster sister. One night my foster sister made me a dinner plate of black-eyed peas and ham where she poured green Pine-Sol detergent in the black-eyed peas. She informed me that if I did not eat it, they were going to take me down to the basement more and more. Naturally, I started crying. My foster parents were upstairs and my brothers were outside somewhere. Just as I took one spoonful of the black-eyed peas mixed with the detergent, my foster mother came downstairs and into the kitchen. My foster mother saw that I was crying. She looked at my dinner plate and noticed the green color mixed in my dinner. She asked my foster sister 'what was that'? Of course she did not say anything. After my foster mother sniffed the plate, she asked me how much did I eat? I told her I had only one spoonful. My foster mother snatched my foster sister and dragged her upstairs and beat her senseless. By the Grace of God I had no ill effect from the Pine-Sol detergent. I must say that I never was taken to the basement and tortured again in that form. The torture came next in a very much different way.

About the third and fourth year of my being in the foster home, I began being blamed for things I did not do, such as stealing money off the dresser in my foster parent's bedroom and taking things like watches and other expensive items. My foster father served in the army in WWI. He would make me stand in the corner on my tippy toes over half the night - sometimes all night when I did not have to go to school the next day.

There was a time my foster father took a walking cane and hit me in the head. One time he did that and my head started bleeding. All he did was put a cold wash cloth on my head and told me to go lay down. Other times I was beaten with switches and a very thick leather belt for the things I was being accused of. At that point and time in my life, I truly wanted to just die. I truly hated life itself!!

One summer I went to camp in Delaware. There life revealed to me sex in a very evil form. One of the boys there who literally was twice my size molested me. After that had happened another boy felt that he could just pick on me at will until one of the other guys in camp took up for me and beat the crap out of the bully. I must say that was a good feeling having someone come to my rescue like a big brother. From that single incident I began to feel that life really was not all that bad. The big boy that was twice my size tried to mess with me again until my big-brother friend came to my rescue 'again'. After that I did not have any more problems in camp. During the sexual encounter I was truly lucky the boy's penis never penetrated my rectum (he just humped on me with it).

Going to camp was good for me because I did learn some things about myself such as, being very shy around girls as the camp was co-ed. The camp had dance parties and I found myself too shy to ask one of the girls to dance with me. I also learned that I was going to be a great lover of music. To this very day, music is a part of my life.

In camp I rode a horse for the first time. As I was riding the horse, the horse bucked and through me off onto the ground and by the Grace of God, I was not hurt. I had another encounter with a horse. I was intrigued with the physical make-up of a horse, so I took the liberty to stare in the eyes of a horse. The horse promptly bit me on the chest. From that day forward, I never – ever stared at a horse again unless the horse was on television.

I also learned that I was going to be very athletic because of my great love for sports; football, baseball, soccer, tennis and basketball. God has blessed this body with the ability to do it all. Now after the two-week camp was over, I went back home to more of the same thing – being teased about my looks and being picked on daily by the neighborhood bully until my younger foster brother found out about it and made me fight him. To my surprise I beat him. I was told to keep rushing at him and do not stop until the bully was on the ground. So I did!! After that day I had much respect in the neighborhood. I began to have good relationships with all the kids in the neighborhood.

CHAPTER THREE

During the year of 1968 life had dealt me a devastating blow. I lost my foster mother. She had gone to the hospital for what reason I did not know. I remember going to the hospital to visit her with my foster father. We talked and before I left, she kissed me and I kissed her. The very next morning she was gone. I felt that my whole world had come crashing down around me. When I was informed of her death the only thing or the only memory I could think of was she took me to church one time and that I fell asleep. During the evening of her death, my older foster brother informed me that she had a blood clot on her heart. After the funeral I remember coming home and crying myself to sleep. After the passing of my foster mother, I began making life very difficult for myself by going out to play and coming back after dark when I was told to come in the house before dark – that prompted a beating. Getting caught stealing and being put out of the 7-11 convenience store prompted another severe beating.

When the manager would not allow me to come in the store, I would stand outside and beg people to go in the store for me, especially when my foster father would send me to the store for something. After I was finally allowed back in the store, I began to be more focused on my schooling or education. I must say that is something I truly wanted – a really good education!

During this time of my life when I was getting ready to graduate from elementary school, I often found myself reflecting on what life had revealed to me and how life itself was shaping and molding me as a human being.

Life had showed me that people in general have no regard for human life. For example: the Kennedy assassinations, the Martin Luther King assassination, and the Vietnam War. At that time I had a great heaviness upon my heart because there was nothing I could do about it.

Life had also revealed to me the sexual indecency that is in the hearts of some people; for example, my camp experiences (a boy wanting to have sex with another boy). Life had also revealed to me that some people had genuine love in their hearts; for example, my foster mother, the big brother friend I had met in camp and some of my classmates in school.

I knew that this thing called life was going to be a bumpy ride and that I was in this for the long haul. When I graduated from elementary school, I felt a sense of accomplishment and that made me feel very proud and special.

During the summer of 1971 I did something that would change my life forever. I saw some old army lapel pins lying around the house. Wearing pins on your clothes was the style at that time, so I promptly took them without asking my foster father for them. To make more friends I gave some of the pins away. When my foster father found out he was very furious. He told me that I had better get outside and get all of his pins back. I managed to get all of them except one as one of the kids had lost it or at least that is what he told me. I was truly scared to death to go back home without all of them. I felt that he would have beaten me senseless. So, I did not go back home for close to a week and a half. During that time I was gone no one came looking for me at all. My friends would bring me food and I would sleep in their parent's cars. Finally, I overcame my fear and went back home. I gave my foster father all the pins except that one. He did not beat me. He just informed me that I must leave his home.

He called the welfare department and they put me in a group home for boys. The name of the group home was N.I.I. which means National Involvement Institute. I just knew I was getting ready to learn a lot about life. The counselors there were really nice to me and they made me feel right at home. In the beginning things were going well for me. I had started my first year of junior high school which was in the same area I grew up in near my foster parent's home. So, I basically knew half the student in school. At times I would lay in my bed at night and think about my foster brothers and sister, wishing I was with them. I truly missed them a lot. Now during my stay at the group home I managed to build good relationships with most of the guys. It was at this point in time of my life I was introduced to drugs and alcohol. Life had revealed to me the instruments of evil. Then, I started smoking cigarettes and headed down a road of destruction.

CHAPTER FOUR

I had built a strong friendship with one of the guys in the group home. We just seemed to click right from the start. It seemed to me that he was the head guy there as he was the oldest and tallest. He was a dark skinned fellow about six foot two or three, had a very nice personality, and he was like a big brother to me. During my first year of junior high school, about four or five of my friends around the way (which means the area I grew up in) would meet over at a friend's house about forty-five minutes before school and smoke pot. In spite of my getting high I always managed to get my school work done. Several times we all cut classes and stayed at one of my friend's house and just got high all day long.

When we would cut class, a lot of the times we would get someone to go in the store for us to get some beer. There were times we experimented with acid (yellow sunshine, window pane, and others I can not remember at this time). During this period in my life, I found myself going to class and acting a fool. Just laughing for no apparent reason and sometimes not doing my homework. I was doing just enough to get by and I knew that was not good. When

I came back to my senses somewhat, I slowed down from getting high.

As my shyness began to be going away, I started taking a stronger interest in girls and found myself dating on a regular basis. My first sexual encounter was with a woman twice my age. I felt that was good, because I did not know what I was doing at all. Life had revealed to me that sex felt really good.

During my first year at the group home, I really started to focus on my school work simply because I knew if I wanted to get ahead in life, I had to have a good education. Things went quite well for me for the first two years at the group home. I was getting my school work done, and I was passing to the next grade with no problem.

About the third year my best friend (that tall fellow who was like a brother to me) had to leave because when you turned eighteen, they let you loose. I was terribly hurt he was leaving. Life had finally showed me that I was capable of loving others. Well, we said our goodbyes and we've never seen each other since. Even to this day I often think about him and how he is doing.

Life was about to show me a new form of evil – jealousy. As I continued to go to school to get a proper education, girls were becoming more and more desirable to me. I was fascinated with their physical make-up especially their breast. I was beginning to think of myself as being a lady's man. At one point I had three girlfriends at one time. I truly did not plan it to happen, things just happened. I learned the hard way that this was not cool at all because one of them gave me VD (venereal disease). At first I did not even know who gave it to me but later on down the road I did in fact find out who did. Needless-to-say she was cut off in a hurry. Another situation had arisen when two of my girl friends showed up at the group home about ten minutes apart. That was an experience I care not to ever go through again.

CHAPTER FIVE

Due to my sexual activities, even though life had showed me that it was not cool at all, did I take heed? No, not at all! I continued down the same path of evil. I managed not to catch another disease until later down the road. I continued to fancy myself a lady's man. It was getting to the point that I had an obsession. Every time I turned around I had a different girl. Sneaking the girls upstairs to my bedroom and having big-time sex so I thought. Some of the guys in the group home were getting more and more jealous. They were already jealous from the relationship that my best friend (the tall fellow) and I had and by them seeing me with all of these girls which only just compounded the envy in their hearts. They started planning these little meetings. Every time I turned around I was the topic of discussion. They started jumping me and by the grace of the living and true God, I was always able to protect myself (my face) from sustaining any marks or scares.

This went on for a few months until one of the counselors saw what was going on. The counselor stood right at the door looking at the guys jump me with a smile on his face. I will never forget that smile. It was almost like he enjoyed seeing the guys inflicting pain on me. He promptly brought an end to it when he saw one of the guys slam his foot down on my head as I was lying on the floor. To my delight the meetings finally came to an abrupt end. A few weeks later a girl's group home opened; and yes, I went through there like a cyclone hungry for sex.

CHAPTER SIX

During this trying time I managed to continue my education. At this point I finally met a girl at the group home that was very special to me. We had such a great time with one another. She was about 5'6", weighted about 130 pounds with a size 38" breast cup. She was all I wanted and yes, at that point I became a one-woman man. I was settling down in my ways, for a little while anyway. I was about to graduate from Jr. High School and my girl friend and I went to the prom and it was absolutely beautiful. One of the counselors at the group home had chauffeured us to the prom in his gray and black Eldorado car. We truly had such a beautiful time. The prom was one of the highlights of my life.

My first year of high school was somewhat boring. I really did not have a drive or desire to continue my education until one of the guys that I went to junior high school with moved into the group home with his older brother when something had happened at his house. I believe he mentioned that they had a fire of some sort. Our friendship grew very strong. We were very competitive in everything from football, to baseball and to basketball; especially basketball as we played that more than anything else.

We would also get high together. Yes, my drug use picked up more when he moved in. I remember when one of the counselors invited a few hand-picked guys from the group home to his farm which was way out in Maryland I believe. It was there he introduced us to Angel Dust. I felt that I was in another world and could not walk normally. I felt that I was walking or trying to walk on clouds. It was truly such an abnormal feeling. It was a feeling that I care not to ever experience ever again in this life that is for sure.

My best friend at this time was about my size (5'10" and about 145 pounds). The only difference was that he was very light skinned while I was dark skinned; and I felt he was better looking than me. His brother too was both very friendly and quite handsome. The brother was medium build, his complexion was between light and dark, and he had hazel eyes. The girls loved them both, and I admit that I was somewhat envious. However, I still had my share of woman for sure.

My girlfriend from the group home and I were not seeing very much of each other. I was going to school and spending more time with my best friend from junior high who now lived at the group home. It came to the point where my girl friend and I just stop seeing one another. About one year later I remembered seeing her walking down the street with a group of people. I am not sure where I was going but she came over to me and stated, "Do you know that Jesus is coming soon?" (quote) I looked at her like she was crazy. She said, "Really" and I said "OK, you take it easy". From that point on I always kept that thought in my mind even to this day and I am very thankful for it.

At this point in my life, time was growing short for my stay at the group home. I continued going to school which was named Cardoza High School and it was there that I met the mother of my daughter. We dated until I had to leave the group home. I must say that I never ever enjoyed sex the way I enjoyed it with her. She truly opened my eyes to a love making experience.

Chapter Seven

When the time came for me to finally leave the group home, I was in my last year of high school, and I had not planned anything as far as where I was going to live. You might say that I was irresponsible which in fact I was because I was used to being cared for. I never had to provide my own food, transportation, money, or medical needs, etc. Life was about to show me how tough it is being on my own and enduring the consequences of the choices I make in this thing called life that I had been ushered into from birth.

The counselors had a meeting to discuss what they were going to do with me. One of the counselors volunteered to let me stay with him. I was truly grateful for his kindness; however, I knew it was going to come with a price and it did! When I moved in, I was truly uncomfortable because of the neighborhood. The counselor lived on the other side of town in the northeast side of Washington, D.C. and to make matters worse, I found out that the counselor was gay.

During this unsettling time, I managed to continue going to school and have a relationship with my future daughter's mother. My best male friend at the group home and I continued to see each other at school until he and his brother moved from the group home and into their place in Bladensburg, MD. About a month later the counselor I was staying with attacked and tried to sexually rape me. He even put his nasty tongue in my ear. So, I promptly pushed him off me and begged him not to ever do that again. I did not want to bring physical violence upon him because he was allowing me to stay in his household. He informed me soon after that he wanted me to leave if I would not have sex with him. Life was continuing to show me how evil this world really is. At this point the counselor informed me I had to move even though I was really sick with a very bad cold. I asked him if I could stay there until I was over my cold and he said, "No". So, when I called my best friend in Maryland and informed him what had happened, he and his brother said that it was OK for me to stay with them.

During this time, I continued seeing my girl friend more and more and going to school less and less. She, her mother, two brothers and two sisters all moved to Alexandria, VA. She also had two other sisters who were already out on their own. During my stay with my best friend in Maryland, I felt out of place simply because they were getting high every day and having a lot of women over the house. It got to a point where I was not going to school anymore. I did not like the life I was living, so I begged my girl friend's mother until I finally convinced her to let me move into their huge house.

I was truly thankful they let me stay with them for a while. There were no problems and all of us were getting along just fine until the oldest brother tried to rape my girlfriend (his sister)! I was watching TV and decided to go upstairs to see what was keeping her. She was sitting on her bed crying. When I asked her what the problem was, she told me what had happened. The brother had locked himself in the bathroom. When I shouted at him to bring his butt out of the bathroom so I could crack his head wide open, he never came out. So, my girl friend and I told her mother what had happened. To my surprise she did not believe it and did not want anything else to be said or done concerning the situation.

This was not a good point and time in my life as I clearly did not like what life was showing me. I felt in my heart that there was nothing but evil in this world and that no one was meant to be happy.

CHAPTER EIGHT

After a few months passed, it finally happened. My girl friend became pregnant with my daughter. Even though my girl friend's mother was truly mad, she agreed to let me stay under her roof until the baby was born on February 19, 1977. She was a healthy seven and a half pounds of pure beauty. I was truly happy at that point in my life. My girl friend's mother allowed me to stay in her household until my daughter was one year old. During that time, I was doing various cleaning jobs at people's homes and also some yard work.

In the process I finally found a room to rent at a rooming house and had found a steady job at W & J Sloanes Furniture Store in Shirlington, VA. Things were going well until I came home to find that someone had broken into my place and stole my money from under my mattress. Just another time life had dealt evil unto me.

CHAPTER NINE

The rooming house I was staying in was really old and was not kept up very well. The people who were staying there were much older than I was. There were quite a few alcoholics staying there too. So, I promptly found another rooming house in Alexandria, VA. That house was old too; however, it was a lot cleaner, had only one tenant and at least I knew my belongings would be safe.

At this point in my life I was still working at the furniture store and managing my relationship with my daughter and her mother. In my heart I felt something was missing; that something was friends such as guys to go out with and play ball. As far as my best friend in Maryland, he and his brother had moved so I lost all contact with them. I started going out playing basketball and meeting new people. Then I started drinking beer on a regular basis and smoking weed. One night I came home and boiled some eggs and fell asleep. When I woke up the house was filled with smoke and a terrible smell. After I aired the house out the next day, I understood when my landlord informed me that I had to move.

I was truly happy I managed to find another rooming house in which I was the only tenant. I was beginning to think that life really was not that bad after all. After a few months at my new place of residence, I was having such a great time playing basketball, and I was playing at the top of my game. As I jumped up for a lay-up shot, I came down wrong on my ankle. When I made it to the Alexandria Hospital, I found out that I had chipped a bone in my ankle. It was truly painful and I could not work for a few weeks. To make matters worse I found out that my girl friend and her family along with my daughter were moving to Woodbridge, VA. I was truly hurt for a long time - for a few months to be exact. After a few weeks, I went back to the hospital to do a follow-up visit with the doctor concerning my ankle. It had healed nicely. After finishing with the doctor something told me to put in an application for a job. About a week later I was hired in housekeeping - that was in 1979.

In 1979 while working at the hospital in Alexandria, VA, I was meeting a lot of new friends, especially women. I was going through women like termites eating through wood. After I had met and become good friends with a tall young man at the hospital, we decided to get our own place not too far from the hospital. We both had our share of women. At this point I was not seeing my daughter or her mother as much as I would have liked. Sad to say, I did not care.

My roommate had met a guy that did not work at the hospital. When we were off work at the hospital, we would drive around in the new friend's car picking up women and bringing them to the house to have orgies. This went on for a few years, getting high on weed and drinking beer. Then my best friend (roommate) and I got tired of the lifestyle we were living. So, we decided to each move into his own place. He moved into a one bedroom apartment and I moved into an efficiency apartment. We continued to play ball and hang out playing cards, getting high and drinking beer. During this time I did continue to see my daughter's mother off and on; however, not as much as I would have liked. By me not being the father to my daughter that I would have liked to be and not seeing my daughter's mother as much as I would have liked, I started focusing on things like getting high and seeing other women. I became bored after a couple of years of living the same thing over and over again, and I felt I needed a change in my life.

Life was showing me that I would never experience true happiness with the lifestyle I was living. I wanted a full-time woman in my life. At this point I guess I had been at the hospital for about three to four years now when I met a woman there that I felt would add purpose to my life. Without hesitation, I promptly introduced myself to her. She was so pretty; moreover, she was about 5'6", and 125 pounds with a breast size of at least 38 double D. I learned that she was from Panama and that she already had a little girl who was about 3 years old. While working at the hospital as a student nurse, she continued her studies to become a nurse. I must admit she looked very good in her student nurses uniform. We continued to get to know one another and became very good friends. Even though we were both very shy, we managed to have great sex with one another. We truly enjoyed each other's company and more importantly her daughter and I got along with each other very well.

CHAPTER TEN

Now after dating for about six months my lady friend and I decided to get a place together. The place where we wanted to move to was very big and beautiful. To my surprise the manager informed us that we had to be married in order for us to move in. So, we promptly went to the hospital and had our blood tests done and went to the justice of the piece and became man and wife.

Life was about to show me the struggles of marriage. Why struggle you might ask? Simply because I did not personally marry her out of love but only to be able to move into our new home or apartment.

After being married for a few months, things were going very well. I had a desire to meet her mother and father. She informed me that before we moved in with each other, she was staying with her mother and that her father had passed away. So, I really never pursued seeing or meeting her mother. I figured she would have me meet her when she was ready.

During this time I had transferred to the operating room as a nurse's assistant. My duties consisted of cleaning the operating rooms after surgery, prepping or shaving males for their various operations such as hernia, arthroscopic knee surgery, etc., and transporting patients to and from the operating room.

Now, my new wife was working part-time at the Woodbine Nursing Home as well as studying to become an LPN. One of the nurses I worked with in the operating room knew the lady that I had just married because she had worked with her at the nursing home. She, meaning the nurse that I worked with in the operating room, informed me that my wife actually was not living her mom, but had lived with the maintenance man at the nursing home and was still driving his car. When I confronted my wife concerning this matter, she admitted that it was true and that she was sorry for lying to me. From that point on I knew I would have a hard time trusting women. Life had showed me that even women can be very deceitful. In spite of my feelings I managed to forgive her and love her faithfully as much as I could. She informed me that the maintenance man was old enough to be her grandfather and that she was only with him to use him for what she could get. In my heart I felt that she was very wrong for that and that she may be just using me to get her green card. However, I never confronted her about that as we continued to be together. Our relationship became stronger and we were having a wonderful time with one another. My step daughter and I too were having a wonderful time with each other. She also respected me as if I was her real or biological father and I really appreciated it.

I was beginning to feel that I had a real purpose in life. During this time my friends at work and I started hanging out getting high more and more. I found myself spending money foolishly on drugs (weed) and beer and just being irresponsible as a husband and parent. Then it happened that my wife was pregnant with my son. Great joy came upon me. I was really looking forward to having a son. That slowed me down from hanging out with my friends.

Chapter Eleven

The birth of my son went very well. The doctors said my son was a '10' – meaning no complications and that he was a seven pound ten ounce baby boy. On the day of delivery I was working in the operating room and was permitted to go up to the labor and delivery room after the birth of my son. Life had given me my very own family, and I did not know what to do with myself. I continued to work at the hospital even though I was getting tired of working there.

I started cheating on my wife and getting high more and more. One night I had a sexual encounter with a woman in my car. The next day I realized that I had the rent money in the glove box or the trunk. I was not sure what had happened to it. A few months later my family and I were evicted from the apartment. That was one of the lowest points of my life so far and so very embarrassing having all of our clothes, furniture and personal belongs thrown outside on the sidewalk. I felt less than a man allowing this to happen to my family. By the grace of God I managed to get some money and rented a U-Haul truck to move and put our furniture and other items of importance in a storage unit.

My wife and kids went to stay with my wife's mother and I went to stay with my daughter's mother who had just gotten her own place in Alexandria, VA. However, she did not want anything to do with me sexually. I was very happy she let me stay with her until I was able to get another place for my family.

About a month later my wife was able to find a very nice place for us; however, a lot smaller than the apartment we were evicted from. Life had given us another chance.

CHAPTER TWELVE

My wife and I picked up where we left off and things were going quite well, except that I was growing weary working at the hospital. However, I hung in there for the sake of my family. I would say I had been at the hospital for about five years. Life was about to bring a physical blow upon me. For some reason when I would have a bowel movement I would bleed from my rectum and at times it was very heavy. I learned that I had a severe case of hemorrhoids which was very unpleasant. I took off from work and had an operation at Howard University Hospital which went very well. I then started having a problem with my lower back. I come to find out that the anesthesiologist broke the needle off in my back when he was trying to give me an epidural to numb me from the waste down. I had to stay in the hospital for a few extra days. When I finally went home, I had to go back into the hospital due to the constant pain in my lower back when the problem was finally corrected. I felt that I could have sued the doctor for his negligence; however, I let it go. I was not charged anything for the operation.

So life goes on. I continue to be a loving husband and father for about another year. Then I met a young lady that lived down on the second floor of the same apartment building my family and I lived. I had a short relationship with her until my family and I moved from the apartment and began renting a much better home located in Alexandria, VA. I continued to grow more and more weary of working at the hospital due to the nurses not informing us when the patients were in isolation and when we would come up to transport them to the operating room. When a patent is in isolation, we are to put on gloves, cap, mask and gowns before entering the room. That would truly frustrate me to no end. There were some very prejudice doctors who would not speak when I would greet them with a 'Good Morning' or 'How are you'? I was truly fed up. Life was showing me more evil in the form of prejudice and bigotry. In the meantime my wife had become a nurse and started working at the Goodwin House Nursing Home getting paid very good money.

During this time I would think about my daughter who lived in Woodbridge, VA. My daughter's grandmother started working at the hospital part-time. So, I was able to communicate with my daughter more. I also had my daughter come over and spend some weekends with my family during the summer. We had such a great time; it was a beautiful thing to behold. Life was showing me things can be very delightful when you are being faithful and loving toward your family.

At this time my family and I continued going out to picnics, movies, visiting friends, just basically doing the things families should do. My son who was about two or three now was getting bigger every day. After working at the hospital about seven years, I was so tired of it, I just up and quit. I walked out and never showed my face there again until a few years later when I decided to go visit a few of my friends.

I had found a job working at the United States Parachute Association as a mail clerk/store manager. My job consisted of going back and forth to the Post Office and mailing out publications and awards to the members.

CHAPTER THIRTEEN

During this period in my life, things were going well with my family. I was seeing my daughter every now and then but not as much as I would have liked. At least I was seeing her and things were going very well. I just could not be content with the way the things were. Life had showed me that I have things in my heart that were just plain evil such as going out continuing to have sexual pleasures with other women, continuing to hang out with the fellows getting high and neglecting my responsibilities of my family.

One of the women I met had introduced me to crack cocaine. That was the beginning of my end. The lady told me not to ever use the drug even though she was using it. She informed me of some of the things crack had done to others. She said that she was strong enough for it not to ruin her life. Did I listen? No!!! I regret every minute too. Even to this day I truly regret it. Life was about to show me what life is all about when you go down the path of crack cocaine. Please believe me my dear brothers and sisters; it is a path of utter destruction. TAKE IT FROM ONE WHO KNOWS!

I am going to share with you my adventures in the life of crack cocaine. The care of family matters became nonexistent. I started lying to my wife for the reasons I was coming home late. At that time she was working eleven at night to seven in the morning. Most of the time I managed to make it home to ensure the kids were in bed. However, I was leaving two very young kids in a big house all by themselves. By the grace of God nothing never happened to them.

My wife and I managed to have two cars which made it possible for me to go down that path in a more rapid pace by having women to give me oral sex while I smoked crack from a glass pipe. I started missing time from work due to hanging out all night. I started losing weight due to not eating. First it started out as two or three day binges. Then it came to the point every time I was able to get money, I was gone from the house for one or two days at a time. My eyes were looking like they were sunk into my head. I was beginning to look horrible; however, I did not care. It was to the point I had to wear a pair of shorts in order for my pants to fit. Then, the inevitable happened. I started taking money out of my wife's bank account for my crack addiction and YES, I did not care. It had come to the point that the only thing I cared about was where I was going to get more money for crack. Brothers and sisters crack had become my God.

One of my job functions was to go to the Post Office to deliver the mail. After leaving the Post Office, I pulled off the road to smoke some crack before going back to the Parachute Association. I knew then it had gone way beyond my control. So, I just quit my job and started selling crack to support my habit. While I was going further down this path of destruction, I always felt that the worst thing that could happen to me was to get arrested. I come to find out that it was the best thing that could have ever happened to me. Yes, my beloveds I was finally arrested and went directly to jail. The reason for my arrest was possession of a controlled substance with intent to distribute. After being locked up for about three weeks, my wife came and paid my bond to get me out of jail.

After being bonded out of jail, I managed to stay clean and sober for a while or at least until my court date and the proceedings were over. Since it was my first offense the judge went very easy on me and just gave me time served and a fine. After that I managed to keep my nose clean for a while. I found a job working at Seven Eleven as a cashier and then later became Assistant Manager. I found a better job working at the Marriott Hotel as a Security Officer. At the same time I also became a Bellman and van driver. After about a month I became a full-time Bellman and van driver. I was averaging about a hundred dollars a day in tips alone. I bought a lockbox and was storing all my tip money in that box. That money was looking so good. One night on my way home from work I took it upon myself to go in town to find a woman to give me oral sex for some crack. When I saw her smoking it, the urges came right back and before you know it, I was smoking too. I went home and took the rest of my money out of the lock box and started at it again.

My wife was still working the eleven to seven shift at night, so I managed to get away with it this time. I built up my money again and this time there was no return. After the money was gone, I started giving people rides for money so I could get more crack. After all I took my family through; I was back at it again. You see my beloveds the insanity in this addiction? I continued down this path of evil – a life of utter destruction. The sad and hurtful part of it all, I had no remorse for what I was doing to my family. I never went back to the hotel, and I never called to let them know I was not coming to work. My life was in complete shambles, and I did not know what to do but go back out and get more crack. I was very successful at getting money by giving people rides. In the process I met people that wanted to smoke crack just as much as I did. At one point I was up for seven days in a row with not going to sleep. Finally, my body just crashed. I fell asleep in my car for about seven or eight hours. When I awoke I started the madness all over again. I was wearing the same clothes day after day and I could care less. My body was wearing down. However, I refused to acknowledge it. I continued in my mission of utter destruction. I finally went back home while my wife and kids were gone, changed clothes, grabbed some food, and went back at it. After another week of this madness, I had received enough money to start selling crack. I was so stoned at this point that I did not even care to look around before I stepped out of my car to make the sale. I just did not care. Yes, it was the police, and I was arrested again! I knew that I was going to see some jail time. In my heart I knew I needed help but I did not know where I was going to get it. I was arrested for the same thing as before – possession of a controlled substance with intent to distribute. I informed my wife of my arrest so she could get the car. My wife was very happy I was arrested so I could get help. I was in jail for six months. During my stay I was in population for one month and the last five months I was in a drug program that was inside the jail. The name of the program was the Sober Living Unit. There I was introduced to NA&AA.

CHAPTER FOURTEEN

Since this was the first time I was jailed for this length of time, I would like to share with you my experiences. Being in population showed me just how wicked the heart can be. I met men that did not have any regard for other human beings. I saw men beat up for their dessert. I witnessed men getting into fights over a meaningless card game. I have seen men taken advantaged of because of their size. I also witnessed men and young teenagers being sexually abused. Life had revealed to me just how unpleasant life can be behind bars. I was one unhappy scared individual. However, I did realize that I had brought everything upon myself.

Life also revealed to me that the police or deputies working in the jail have no respect for the prisoners. For example, when you make a request to see the doctor, it is no telling how long it will take. You would have to be half dead to see the doctor right away or at least the same day. I must say that it was an eye opening experience that I will never forget.

Now, I will share with you the five months I spent in the sober living unit. I must say being there was much better than population. I would like to mention one other thing I witnessed in population.

Prisoners have no desire to do anything with their lives, to better themselves, to truly want to make something out of the life they have, and certainly no goals set for themselves. When I saw that it prompted me to start thinking about my life. Did I want to wind up a complete failure; a very poor example to my kids being in and out of jail for the rest of my life; or wind up dead in some gutter?

Being in the sober living unit was also an eye opening experience, truly. I learned so much about myself. I was introduced to NA&AA which means Narcotics Anonymous and Alcoholics Anonymous. In that drug program I basically learned how drugs and alcohol destroys the human body both mentally and physically. Drugs and alcohol disrupts the heart rate, your breathing, your ability to think clearly and to remember things, your short term memory, your speech patterns and that is only the start of what ill effects that drugs and alcohol brings upon the human body. The sober living unit also helps you to get in touch with your inner feelings; it truly helped me in that aspect. This drug program had a session called 'The Hot Seat' and it was something to truly behold. They would set up a circle of chairs then place one chair in the middle of the circle. The person sitting in the middle of the circle would have to sit there with both hands on his knees. You could not cross your arms as they called that being in a defensive position. While you are sitting there, your peers are letting you have it by degrading you in a most awful way. I have seen many go away crying and yes my beloveds I was one that went away crying. I mean I ran up to my cell crying. I thought I was handling everything they were saying until the female counselor had at it with me. One of the things I remember her calling me in which I will never forget was a black skeezer pleasing crack head. They say the truth hurts. Well, I guess that is one of the things I was. One of the main things I learned while I was in that drug program was that I was going through life feeling sorry for myself because I never saw my real mother and father. When those feelings of self pity would come over me, it would be mostly during the holidays like Thanksgiving and Christmas, etc. as those were family times. One of the things that I really enjoyed in the program was that they let men and women from the outside join our NA&AA unit meetings.

They also had a woman's sober living jail program. They allowed women to join the men's program during the NA&AA meetings. It really tickled me when I saw how some of the inmates would try to pretty themselves up when they knew the women would be coming during that day. For example, some of the inmates would use soap to slick down the waves in their hair, leave the soap on, and then put on a stocking cap. I must say that it did work. Yes, that is right my beloveds, I tried it a few times even though it was a lot of work. It is amazing how I allowed women to interrupt what I should be focused on which is being free from that deadly addiction.

The time was drawing near for my departure from jail. I had not really given any thought on what I was going to do once I got out of jail. At night I would often reflect on the good times I had with my family, my prom date experience, my not graduating from high school and most of all how I hurt my family with this ugly crack addition. When I had two months to go, I received a visit from my wife, son and daughter. My wife informed me she had to move but managed to find a very nice apartment located in Alexandria. She also informed me that she was working two jobs and that she had to hire a babysitter for my son.

Chapter Fifteen

When I took a closer look at my son, he had serious scares on his face. My wife informed me that the babysitter left him in the bathroom sitting on the bathroom sink and that he had gone into the medicine cabinet, grabbed a razor and called himself shaving. When it was all said and done, he had cut his face really bad. I was so mad and hurt I started crying like an over-grown baby. Those scares he has will be with him for the rest of his life. I informed my wife that I was going to hunt that babysitter down and kill her. I was really feeling sorry for myself after that because I knew if I had not been in jail it would not have ever happened. So, I was partly if not all the blame for that incident happening to my son. The babysitter was my wife's cousin and little did I know that I would run into her a couple of years later working at McDonalds. However, I did nothing nor did I say anything to her concerning the incident with my son. My son was with me when I saw her and when I started to say something my son begged me not to.

About the time I had about a month left to go in jail, I was given a court hearing. I was set up with a case worker, given a three year probation period, and ordered to go directly into a drug program as soon as I was released from jail. My case worker was a very nice and attractive lady and I mean really attractive. I shared with her my experiences I endured staying with my foster family and the group home. She informed me that I was a major miracle to have been through all that I had been through and to be able to hold it together the way that I had thus far. Moreover, it is a victory all in itself,

CHAPTER SIXTEEN

Finally, the time had come for me to depart from jail. I must say the main thing that I took from this experience was that I did want to make something of myself. My counselor informed me that she enrolled me in a three month drug program called 'The Pheonix House'. I called my wife and informed her that I was on my way to her new place of residence to pick up some clothes and toiletries. She promptly informed me that she wanted the counselor to come to the door because she allowed her new boyfriend to move in. That was a blow to my heart. It felt as if someone had driven a stake through my heart. In spite of the way I felt I pressed on. The counselor picked up my belongings then dropped me off at the drug program located in Arlington, VA.

Basically, that program was really no different from the sober living unit as far as the knowledge they conveyed to the men and women that were in the program. And, yes the program was co-ed which was a joy. They did not have hot seat sessions and I cannot say that I missed them either. The different things that went on in that program were that men and women had relationships on the side and the amount of food they fed you. When I left jail I weighted about

145 pounds and after I finished the program I weighed about 165 to 170 pounds. They also had a lot of NA&AA meetings at night. About twice a week they would take us on the bus to meetings in Washington, D.C. or somewhere in Virginia.

During the day rap sessions I found myself talking about how bad I felt that I had allowed myself to be controlled by crack cocaine. I also shared about how I felt about my wife having another man in her life, how I was an irresponsible husband and father to my kids, and my feelings about never seeing my real mother and father. I did share that when I was at the group home, the administrator of the home found out that my real mother gave birth to me when she was only fifteen years old. I guess that explains why she was not allowed to keep me. Several years later I tried to pursue finding my real mother without any success at all. I just gave up; even to this day I desire so much to physically meet my biological mother. It has always been hard for me to open up to others about my true feelings. For many years of this life I have been living, I have been suppressing my feelings and been so afraid to tell others how I felt about them or how I felt about certain situations. After being in this program for three months, it did help me to open up to others just a little.

When I had reached the third and final month of the program, they called it the transitional period where you were allowed to go out and find a job. One other thing that was commanded of you was to get a sponsor. A sponsor is a person that has years of being clean and sober. We were ordered to call our sponsor on a regular basis. My sponsor was a middle-aged fellow with about six years clean time. He was about 5'7" and about 140 pounds of pure kindness and gentleness. He was an encouragement in my life. He helped me to get a job working with him. The company was called Termite Control. It was a pretty nice job except when I had to go down into the crawl spaces – meaning having to crawl under people's houses. That truly was an experience to behold.

CHAPTER SEVENTEEN

The time had come for me to leave the drug program, I called my case worker from the jail and informed her of my situation of having had successfully completed the program. From this point I was ordered to live in a halfway house named Frank Young House. This house was basically a 90 day after-care program for addicts. They allowed you to work and when you got paid, you handed them your pay check so that you would have enough money to move into your own place after the 90 days were up.

Another stipulation was that you had to attend an NA&AA meeting five nights out of the week. I was keeping in contact with my sponsor, going to work, and attending my meetings on a regular basis. After about a month and a half, I took the liberty to cash my check, go home to change my clothes, and inform the counselors that I was going to a meeting. Instead, I went to Old Town Alexandria, hooked up with a crack head female, started getting high and had oral sex done on me. Can you believe I did that - after all the education, lectures, wearing a jump suit that said 'prisoner' on the back of it, wearing underwear in jail that many other prisoners had worn and worst yet having the potential of being put right back in jail because of my three year probation period. My case worker had told me that if I did anything to break the law within that three year period, I would be sent directly back to jail. When I went back home I knew I was in trouble. I arrived back about 11:50 pm which was 50 minutes late. When the counselors asked me what happened, I told them the truth. They told me to go to bed and they would be contacting my case worker in the morning. When I went upstairs to my room my mind was racing with all kinds of thoughts. I went into manipulation mode – one of the things I learned from the drug program is that addicts can be very manipulative. I promptly wrote a letter to my case worker stating to please forgive me for what I had done and that I am not jail material. I never robbed a bank or killed anyone. My case worker came to the house, read the letter I wrote and behold she gave me another chance. However, she did inform me that she was going to take me out of the halfway house and put me in the Salvation Army which was another drug program. I thanked her with all my heart because I truly did not want to go back to jail; especially, for three years.

I was at the halfway house for about a week when I called my wife to see how everyone was doing, mainly my son. My wife brought my son to the house to visit with me for a while. I promptly informed them of my situation and told them where I was going. It brought great joy to see my son again even though I mourned in my heart when I looked upon the scares that were on his face. Well, I guess it is to remind me of the evil path I was going down. A few days before I was to go to the Salvation Army, I was up in my head about what should I expect from the program that I was headed to.

Little did I know that my life as I knew it would be forever changed. My heart ached to know what it would take for me to stop doing things that I knew would hurt me as well as those I truly loved. To be honest with you, I did not know how to love others much less how to allow others to love me in return.

The day finally came for me to go to the Salvation Army drug program. My case worker came and picked me up. I said my goodbyes to the guys and the counselors at the house. During my stay I really never bonded with any of those guys or the counselors. However, we all did get along with one another.

My first day at the Salvation Army is a day that I will never ever forget for as long as God gives me breath to breathe. The date was July 9th, 1990 and at that time I was thirty-three years old. The same age when Christ Jesus gave his life for the sins of the whole world. I met the assistant Chaplin of the program. He shared with me briefly some of the things the program had to offer. Then, I met the coordinator of the program. I spent several hours completing paperwork and getting filled in on the do's and don'ts of the program. The program was males only which was a good thing – no distraction from women. It was a pretty big building with a huge chapel for church and prayer meetings. I was informed that this was not only a drug program; it was also a spiritual program.

After filling out all of my paperwork and meeting people of various positions in the program, it was time to eat. I was happy because I was truly hungry. At the Salvation Army they fed you extremely well. I came in weighing at least 165 pounds and when I left I had ballooned up to 187 pounds of pure muscle. I received a tour of the building and was surprised the sleeping quarters were so huge.

CHAPTER EIGHTEEN

Each dorm houses about ten beds. Every one had their own lockers.
For some reason I felt right at home immediately. Later on that night
about a little after 10:00 pm, the assistant Chaplin came for me to
go with him to his office and I promptly went with him. There he
shared with me about God. Then he asked me if I believed in God.
I told him yes, only because I knew within my heart man could not
have made the sky, the stars, and make it rain, etc. The Chaplin
said very good, and he went on to share with me about Jesus Christ
and of how he came upon this world to give his life for us wretched
sinners. Everything he was saying to me was sinking in with great
clarity. No one had ever shared with me what I was being told that
night. The only time I heard the name of Jesus was when I saw my
old girlfriend with a group of people. She came over to ask me if I
knew that Jesus was coming back. My reply was looking at her like
she was crazy. The other times I heard the name of Jesus was when
people yelled it out in an angry way – which is blasphemous and a
very meaningless manner of speaking. As the assistant Chaplin went
on he asked me would I like to be born again. After explaining to
me what being born again was and also helping me understand that

I am truly a sinner, I often wondered why did I have a desire to hate others for no reason; why did I desire to put chemicals in my body when I knew it is not good; to just name a few of the things I did that really irritated me to no end. Well, after chatting with the assistant Chaplin, I sincerely gave my life to Christ Jesus. My brothers and sisters, I truly meant it.

CHAPTER NINETEEN

After receiving Jesus Christ into my heart, I really did not know what to expect. When I did it, I did not feel any different. There was no big explosion; however, there was a gradual change taking place in my heart – meaning my speech pattern was changing, I started saying my brother. I started speaking to others with genuine love in my heart. I did not know it, but to my delight it was just happening.

As the weeks went on in this 90 day program, I learned that every one is given a job within the program. My first job was working in brick and brack – that is working on the loading dock separating all the donations given to the Salvation Army. There were a lot of wonderful items being donated especially clothes and shoes. We were allowed to get items for ourselves to keep which was a very good thing and a blessing too. The work was not easy. It was very strenuous work. However, the Lord gave me the strength to endure. Now during this time, I was still going to the NA&AA meetings held in the program. I felt the NA&AA programs were a very good starting point because of its twelve-step program; however, they have some beliefs I do not agree with such as for example – the agnostics are those that do not believe in God. It is shared in the meeting that it is OK to believe in anything – even a light bulb or a door knob. I totally disagree with that, PERIOD. I also learned that in the meetings no one was allowed to talk about Jesus or what the true and living God is doing in your life. Basically, I felt that my hands were tied.

However, I did like the twelve steps of the program.

1. We admitted we were powerless over drugs and alcohol and that our lives had become unmanageable.
2. Came to believe that a power greater than ourselves could restore us to sanity.
3. Made a decision to turn our will and our lives over to the care of God as we understood Him.
4. Made a searching and fearless moral inventory of ourselves.
5. Admitted to God, to ourselves, and to another human being the exact nature of our wrongs.
6. Were entirely ready to have God remove all these defects of character.
7. Humbly asked Him to remove our shortcomings.
8. Made a list of all persons we had harmed, and became willing to make amends to them all.
9. Made direct amends to such people wherever possible, except when to do so would injure them or others.
10. Continued to take personal inventory and when we were wrong promptly admit it.
11. Sought through prayer and meditation to improve our conscious contact with God as we understood Him, praying only for the knowledge of His will for us and the power to carry that out.
12. Having had a spiritual awakening as the result of these steps. We tried to carry this message to addicts, and to practice these principles in all our affairs.

When these steps are put into action, I truly believe a change will come about.

CHAPTER TWENTY

The twelve steps are what I took from the AA and NA meetings, mostly because it made a lot of sense and most of all; seven of the steps are God related. However, one of the steps I do not agree with and that is Step One – admitting that we are powerless. God tells me from his word that: 1. 'I am the vine, ye are the branches: He that abideth in me, and I in him, the same bringeth forth much fruit: for without me ye can do nothing'. (St. John Chapter 15, verse 5). Moreover, it is written in God's holy word that: 2. 'I can do all things through Christ which strengtheneth me'. (Philippians Chapter 4, verse 13). There you have it: The word of God tells me that I am not powerless if I am truly abiding in the Lord Jesus Christ. My brother and sisters that is a big IF as you will see later on in this book.

After about a month into the program, I changed jobs. I was given the opportunity to work on the security staff. My job consisted of working the 11:00 pm to 7:00 am shift at the front desk. It was truly a blessing because that gave me the opportunity to read my bible. I started off reading the King James version. I became somewhat frustrated because I could not understand it clearly. So, I started reading the Living Bible. I shared with the assistant Chaplin my feelings about the King James version. He informed me that I will have problems at first; then, as the Holy Spirit that abides in me it will make me stronger spiritually and that I will begin to understand it with clarity and power. As the weeks passed I was getting much stronger!

So, as I went back to the King James version, I came across a verse in the word of God that knocked me off my feet" 'As it is written; but the anointing which ye have received of him abideth in you, and ye need not that any man teach you: but as the same anointing teacheth you of all things, and is truth, and is no lie, and even as it hath taught you, ye shall abide in Him'. (1 John Chapter 2, verse 27) That scripture told me that I do not have to depend on any man to teach me but that the Holy Spirit that abides within me will surely reveal God's truth in my heart.

That was truly comforting to my heart. Now after working at the front desk for a few weeks, I was caught sleeping with my head on my bible. I was promptly given another job working in one of the stores. The Salvation Army had stores located all over Virginia. I was truly happy because I was given the opportunity to get out and get some fresh air and meet people.

One day I saw my daughter's grandmother. It truly brought great joy to my heart to see her. Later on that week she brought my daughter to see me. That was a blessing and a joy all in itself!

About a week later I met a woman that was so pretty, and she gave me her phone number. We began talking on the phone and became good friends. After being in the program for two months, you are allowed to spend one weekend away. So, I promptly spent the weekend with the young lady I had met. When we mad love that woman loved me like I had never been loved before. However, back in my mind I knew it was not right in God's eyes.

CHAPTER TWENTY ONE

As time went on at the Salvation Army, I was continuing to feed on God's Holy word and going to vespers. Vespers was a 5:50 pm meeting held Monday through Friday in the chapel. It was truly uplifting. We would sing a few hymns from the hymnal and then there was a spiritual message from a speaker. I gained even more knowledge from those lectures. As this went on I felt myself growing. I was even getting a conscious especially when I had sex with the lovely young lady I met. Any other time I would have thought nothing of it. I knew a change had and was coming over me for the better. Unfortunately, I was not taking heed like I should have as you will see later on in this book.

I had been in the program for three months and learned that after the three months you do not have to leave. They allowed you to stay as long as it takes or rather when you are comfortable leaving and are ready to face the world which was really comforting to know. After knowing this, I promptly went out and found a job and was saving some money. I informed the program coordinator that I was ready to leave. The program gives you a small ceremony and a certificate which I thought was very nice. It showed me that they really cared about your personal welfare. Well, I said my goodbyes to everyone and really thanked the assistant Chaplin for all that he did for me and informed him that I would keep in very close contact with him which I did until the Lord took him home. The strange thing was that he was still a very young man when he died. I must say that it truly broke my heart when he left me.

Chapter Twenty Two

After being at the Salvation Army for about four months, I found a rooming house in Alexandria, VA and started working at a popular carry out called 'Little Jims' which was located in Old Town Alexandria – not too far from where I was living.

One of the things I did when I was settled in my new place was to get down on my knees and pray to the true and living God that he lead me to a bible preaching church and sure enough when I was going home from work one evening, I saw a church right on the corner from where I lived only a few minutes away. I went to the door and the door was not locked. I looked in and there were about a handful of people there having bible study. It was on a Tuesday night and I remember like it was yesterday. I peeked in and everyone turned around and looked at me. I promptly closed the door, left and went straight home from my shyness and not being properly dressed as I had just gotten off from work. During my first week at my new place, I paid a visit to my case worker at the jail to inform her how I was doing and to thank her again for putting me in the Salvation Army program. I told her that was the best thing that could have ever happened to me in this life.

That following Sunday I went to that church where I had peeked through the door on Tuesday night and met the pastor and members of that church. At that time I had no idea that the pastor of that church would become like a father figure in my life and what a blessing as even to this day he is still in my life. The name of the church is 'The Ark of Love Baptist Church'. God has and is using that church to help me to grow and mature as a loving servant of the living Lord Jesus Christ. Now the church I was attending was not big in numbers and I often wondered why the church was not growing. God revealed to me that people do not want to hear the work of God but that people just want an emotional feeling through the music and singing.

The pastor of the church was truly preaching the work of God. He did not water down the word of God, and he was not afraid to talk about heaven and hell. Through the years God has given me upon this earth and from my many visits to other churches, I have noticed that the last thing people want to hear is a sermon preached on heaven and hell.

My pastor is a true man of God and about the number of members in the congregation, I have also learned in the word of God as it is written, 'For where two or three are gathered together in my name, there I am in the midst of them'. (Matthew Chapter 18, verse 20) So, by reading that, I was content with the number of members the Ark of Love have and moreover was more focused on carrying out the will that God has laid down for this life he has so freely given me. Now at this time I was wondering what God's will for my life was.

I just continued to work at 'Little Jims' as a cashier, went to church, and stayed away from those that desired to use drugs and alcohol, and talked to the assistant Chaplin of the Salvation Army.

CHAPTER TWENTY THREE

About a year later I finally met a young lady at 'Little Jims' carry out. She was very sweet, about 5'7" tall, about 125 pounds, slim waistline with a breast size of every bit of 38 to 40DDs. I mean she was it for me. We became to be very good friends and I allowed her to take me off of my focus from serving the Lord faithfully. She had her good qualities such as not being a drug user and very interested in having a relationship with the Lord Jesus Christ.

So, after starting a relationship with this young lady, I was content with this life God had so freely given me. At one point I started getting harassed by bill collectors calling me for previous debts I had accumulated while I was with my wife. I told my pastor what was going on with the debt collectors. He and the church gave me money to file bankruptcy so I could become debt free. I felt that I was on top of the world because I was now debt free and managed to buy a car. At that time life was really good and things were going very well for me.

When my three year probationary period was up, I went to see my case worker. She gave me the paperwork to show that I was in fact free from the court system. Just picture that – debt free and free from the court system!! My life was shaping up in such a glorious way and I had the living Lord Jesus Christ to thank for my countless blessings. While all of this was happening I continued going to church, working and having an adulterous relationship with my lady friend.

Chapter Twenty Four

I did not bother to realize that I was still a married man and how God feels about adultery. I did talk with the pastor of the Ark of Love about my relationship I was having. He did inform me what the word of God says about such behavior. Instead of taking heed I continued in my adulterous ways. I did talk to my lady friend about this situation and that I was going to get a divorce. We continued in this relationship and she started going to church with me and getting involved with church activities. Before you knew it she was growing gracefully in the Lord. During this time I was talking with my daughter more and more and on a regular basis. My daughter even spent a weekend with me and went to church. I introduced my daughter to all of the church members; however, I was not ready for her to meet my lady friend because of the fondness I still had for her mother.

As far as my wife, my step-daughter and son, I did not talk with them very much at this point and time in my life. I was not happy about that; however, I dealt with it. I adopted the attitude that – Life Goes On.

After having left the Salvation Army for about four and half years now, things were somewhat normal. I was not quite content with the relationship I was having but I had in my mind things would get better.

What happened next, I was not expecting. I was laid off my job because the owner sold the business and became strictly catering only. I started receiving unemployment checks and in the process started seeking another job.

Two or three months had gone by and my frustration was building up because I still had not found a job. I stopped going to church and told my lady friend to stay away from me until things got better and I meant every word of it too. So, she stayed away as ordered. A few months later my beloved pastor found out exactly where I lived from my girlfriend who still attended church. My pastor came by to visit, to ask me why I had stopped coming to church and to inform me that everybody missed me. I thought to myself, it was good to be missed as that meant they do care for you in most cases. So, I told him of my unhappiness of not being able to find a job and why God was allowing this to happen to me.

My beloved pastor informed me that God allowed things to happen to you only to draw you closer unto Him and that we should learn to trust in Him alone and not in our own strength. You know that made so much sense to me. Moreover, my pastor went on to tell me that unconfessed sins will hinder our blessings more than anything else. At that moment I started reflecting on the adulterous relationship I was having with my lady friend, so from that day forth I developed a prayer life. I do mean a sincere prayer life.

After a few years of being saved and through the power of the Holy Spirit, I came up with a prayer guideline that would encourage others that have a problem in their prayer life and also would broaden their communication with the living and true God.

CHAPTER TWENTY FIVE

The living Lord laid upon my heart to pin down this prayer guideline so I titled it 'prayer tips':

1. Whenever you pray, pray in Jesus name: (reference John Chapter 14, verse 13): 'Whatsoever ye shall ask in my name, that will I do, that the father may be glorified in the son.' Example, when I pray I start off with saying – Dear Heavenly Father I come to you in the name of your son Jesus Christ. (reference John Chapter 14, verse 6): 'Jesus saith unto him, I am the way, the truth, and the life: No man cometh unto the Father but by me.'

2. Thank God for the life He has given you. Thank God for your family, job, home, health, etc. (reference Ephesians Chapter 5, verse 20): 'giving thanks always for all things unto God and the Father in the name of our Lord Jesus Christ.'

3. Confess your sins – unconfessed sins will hinder your prayers from getting answered. (reference 1 John Chapter 1, verses 6 – 9): 'If we say that we have fellowship with Him, and walk in darkness, we lie, and do not the truth:

But if we walk in the light, as He is in the light, we have fellowship one with another, and the blood of Jesus Christ His son cleanseth us from all sin.' If we say that we have no sin, we are deceiving ourselves and the truth is not in us. If we confess our sins, He is faithful and just to forgive us our sins, and to cleanse us from all unrighteousness.

4. Then pray for others such as your family, the president and his staff, co-workers, the police, church members, etc. (reference James Chapter 5, verse 16): 'Confess your faults one to another, and pray one for another, that ye may be healed. The effectual fervent prayer of a righteous man availeth much.' (reference Matthew Chapter 5, verse 44): 'But I say unto you, love your enemies, bless them that curse you, do good to them that hate you, and pray for them which despitefully use you, and persecute you.'

5. Then pray for your needs. Remember not to be selfish. Ask yourself what are your motives for what you are asking your heavenly father for. Is it to bring glory to him or yourself? (reference James Chapter 4, verse 3): 'Ye ask and receive not, because ye ask amiss, that ye may consume it upon your lust.'

6. End your prayer this way: In Jesus Holy Name, AMEN. (reference St. John Chapter 14, verse 14): 'If ye shall ask any thing in my name, I will do it.

Now, at this time of my life that God has so freely given me, I was unemployed for over six months and counting. However, I did start going back to church fellowshipping with my dear brothers and sisters in Christ Jesus. As far as my lady friend and I, we continued to see one another but focused more on growing in the grace and knowledge of our Lord Jesus Christ.

The Lord finally opened the door to a new job. The job was a security officer for the Northern Security Patrol. It was a privately owned business. The owners were very nice, tight with their money but nice. I really did not care as I was just happy to be among the employed again.

CHAPTER TWENTY SIX

Being at the security company was a real experience – a life changing experience if you please. I was the only black gentleman working for the company. The other guys that I worked with were pretty nice except for one. There is always one rotten apple in the bunch so it has been said. During the first week things went somewhat rough due to the way the one security officer (the rotten apple) was training me. Our job consisted of going from site to site memorizing and patrolling at night the parking lot areas of apartment complexes, office buildings and store parking lots. With him driving so fast and me not being familiar with the Falls Church, Vienna and Fairfax areas, I could not possibly remember where I was going.

There were at least seven to eight different sites we went to, so the very next day I informed the owners (my bosses) of this problem. They said that they would talk with the problem officer. So, that night he resorted to talking to me in a nasty way. Well, I said to myself, Lord please give me the strength to deal with this. So, just before we started out on our patrol and heading to the patrol car, I said to him, 'Are you all right?' and then gave him a look that would have scared the entire German army of World War One. His reply was 'Oh yeah, sure, everything is fine.' From that point on I did not have a problem with him any more. In fact we became the best of friends.

I also started meeting some really nice people. At two of the sites we were to patrol was the Goodwin House Nursing Homes (Goodwin House East and West) which were located not very far from the security headquarters. Both were located on Leesburg Pike a few blocks from each other. I thought to myself what a small world we live in. As my wife worked during the 7:00 am to 3:00 pm shift, I did not see her very much except when she worked an extra shift which was 3:00 pm to 11:00 pm shift. My hours were 6:00 pm to 6:00 am which makes for a very long shift. By the loving grace of God he gave me the strength to endure for about four and half years. When we patrolled the nursing homes our job consisted of patrolling the parking lot to deter car vandalism, then foot patrol inside of the building. That is how my wife and I saw one another to both of our surprise. When we spoke I would often ask her about my son. She said that she would keep me informed of his progress as far as his schooling and such. As time went on I continued going to church and going to bible study when I did not have to work. During the process I started getting involved in church duties. First I became an usher, then a Sunday School Superintendent. I found myself even teaching Sunday School. I personally found that to be a serious challenge because I felt within my heart if I am going to stand up in front of the congregation, it was very important for me to be faithful to the Lord in order for me to be an effective bible teacher. Well, as I continued teaching I still continued to have a relationship.

CHAPTER TWENTY SEVEN

After about a year of being at this rooming house, the same place I moved to after leaving the Salvation Army, my lady friend wanted to move out of her mother's house. She was staying with her mother and her two brothers. I am not sure but I think her brothers were around the 19 and 20 age range. I encouraged my lady friend to rent a room in the same rooming house I was staying which was a serious mistake. After she moved in I even got her a job working for the same security company. We were seeing quite a lot of each other and the love we had for one another grew rapidly. We found ourselves spending many nights together in my bed making love. In my heart I knew it was not right, but I was not strong enough to do anything about it.

After a few months of this I told the pastor of the Ark of Love Baptist Church what was going on and that I wanted to step down from being the Sunday School Superintendent and teaching the Sunday School lessons. It truly hurt me to stop but I was tired of being convicted in my heart for the lifestyle that I was living.

After stepping down from my church duties, I continued to be faithful as far as my attendance in church. My lady friend and I continued in our adulterous ways and still went to work and church together. She was working on a site that needed someone there at all times. I continued driving the patrol car to the assigned sites given to me. About a year and half later, I received a promotion.

CHAPTER TWENTY EIGHT

It was a good feeling to get compensated for tireless hours of hard work I put in every day at the security company. Without a doubt I truly could use the extra money for sure. Along with the title of sergeant I now wore white shirts while the others wore grey. I was getting compliments from a lot of females on the sites, especially at the nursing homes. There was one lady that worked at the Goodwin House West site that took a special interest in me when I first started working for the security company. She worked the Friday and Saturday shift from 11:00 pm to 7:00 am. We just talk to each other in the beginning. Little did I know at that time our friendship would grow into something really special later on down the road in this roller coaster of a life I was entrenched in. Even to this day that lady is a very dear friend to me even as I am writing this book.

After receiving my promotion, my lady friend wanted to move from the rooming house and to get our own apartment so we did. We found a pretty nice apartment in Delray another area in Alexandria, VA. Things were going very well for us at that time. We continued going to church and working the same job.

The pastor found out that my lady friend and I were living together and was not pleased with my decision making. With all of his God given might he encouraged me to get out of this relationship and to go back to my wife. I told my pastor that my wife did not want to have anything to do with me. I could not really blame her for not wanting to be with me. At time I really did not want to be with myself either. My pastor informed me that with God all things are possible. I gave that some thought for a very long time that day. I knew something had to be done right away. I told my lady friend about what the pastor said. She did not like the pastor telling me to go back to my wife. I informed her why the pastor said what he said only because of God's feelings about divorce. She understood for a while anyway. I told my lady friend that I was going to tell my wife that I wanted a divorce so we could get married right away.

About a few months later I finally saw my wife. I knew my wife liked what she was seeing of me and what she was hearing from the other nurses that saw me on a regular basis. For some reason I told my wife that you either take me back now or give me a divorce. She put me on hold about a month and to my surprise she told me that she wanted me back. Brothers and sisters I truly did not know what to do. I mean it. I just did not know.

So, I put her on hold for a few months or at least until my current apartment lease expired. After the lease expired my lady friend and I went into our own apartments. Not only did my lady friend get her own place but she started working somewhere else – a place in Burke, VA – the same area I moved to before going back to my wife. My lady friend still was not happy with what the pastor had told me concerning going back to my wife; however, she never talked about it ever again.

CHAPTER TWENTY NINE

At this time I was on a month-to-month lease at the place I was staying. As far as my lady friend, she stopped going to church with me because she knew within her heart what decision I was going to make and she was right.

I finally told her of my decision and she told me that I hurt her very much. When I saw her crying I was totally destroyed for about a month. What gave me the strength to move on of course was God's grace and the fact that my son was spending time with me by spending the weekends at my place.

When my son was coming to my place his hair was not properly groomed and his clothes were not properly cared for the way they should have been and that weighted heavily on my decision. I felt within my heart that my son needed me dearly like all kids need both parents in their lives each and every day. I just did not want to pick up and move back in with my wife because I still had feelings for my lady friend. So, I waited until those feelings eventually went away.

While I was still working at the security company, the friendship started to pick up with the young lady who worked part time at the nursing home on Friday and Saturday. After a few months before I moved back in with my wife, the part-time lady at the nursing home and I went into the first floor bathroom where she started giving me oral sex. I was in a state of confusion because of my extra marital affairs. I did not dare tell my pastor about this affair.

After a few times of this, my friend at the nursing home and I put our sexual affairs on hold because I told her that I was a child of the living Lord Jesus Christ and that I was going back to my wife. She understood and informed me that she was living with a man that treats her very cruelly and that was the reason she allowed herself to perform those sexual acts with me.

After staying in Burke for about three to four months, I called my lady friend I was involved with for the past few years to see if she had any resentment in her heart toward me and to inform her to try not to. She answered the phone and then promptly hung up on me.

When that happened it was like someone had driven a stake through my heart. I happened to be off work that night and took the liberty to go to Washington D.C. to find a woman who smoked crack cocaine. After she showed me where to buy it, we went to a private place where there was no traffic of any sort and she gave me all the oral sex I wanted because I gave her all the crack she wanted.

At that time I did not use crack but the time did come when I did in fact start using crack again. I cannot believe I threw away several years of being clean and sober. This happened about three weeks after my sexual encounter I had with that female I met in D.C. the night I was hung up on by my lady friend. Even though I was using crack again, I was still able to maintain my security job; however, my church attendance had dropped off miserably.

After using crack for about a month I went down on my knees to ask the Lord to please give me the grace to overcome this problem.

CHAPTER THIRTY

After staying away from D.C and those crack-head women, the Lord took the desire away from me and I stayed out of my own destructive ways. It had been about six months since moving to Burke, VA and not using crack for about two months. I felt that I was ready to go back to my wife. She welcomed me back with open arms. The relationship with my beloved son and step daughter grew really strong.

My problem with my wife was mainly in bed as I could not keep an erection. I felt in my heart that it was due to not having a really genuine love in my heart for her. However, I told her it was due to masturbating too much when I was in my own place. She bought it and life went on.

I felt that God had given me a fresh start with my family. I knew it was not going to be easy; however, I knew that life in itself was just a life-long learning experience. The one thing I also knew was that as long as I allowed God to be in control of this life he had blessed me with, I knew things could only get better.

The pastor of the Ark of Love was very happy to see that my wife and I were back together again. The following Sunday after I moved back in with my wife and family, I encouraged them to accompany me to church. I did not force them to go as I had learned over the years that you never force someone to go to church. In order for people to get anything out of church is that they have to desire it within their own hearts and not just do it to please someone else. It would be a miserable waste to themselves as well as to the one they are trying to please. As my family and I went to church that Sunday, I had such a wonderful feeling in my heart and thought to myself that this is the way life should be. The church members welcomed my family with open arms and my family loved going to church. They could see and feel the love that was there.

My wife and I were beginning to really love each other like a husband and wife should love one another. It was a wonderful thing to behold. On my off days from my security job, my son and I would go play basketball with each other every chance we could get.

Life was shaping up to be so wonderful to me. My pastor and I started going out witnessing telling others about Jesus Christ. The Holy Spirit that lives within my heart really started coming alive within me with great power.

My dear brothers and sisters I started having a great time telling others about Christ Jesus every chance the Lord gave me. It was a huge encouragement to me to press on and run the race that was set forth before me when I started seeing others receive Christ into their lives. As it is so written in 1 Corinthians Chapter 9, verse 24: 'Know ye not that they which run in a race run all, but one receiveth the price? So run, that ye may obtain.' The pastor saw the way I was maturing as a servant of the Lord Jesus Christ and pushed me to become a deacon of the church. I was truly very reluctant because I felt that I was not worthy to hold such a title; however, I went through with it anyway.

Chapter Thirty One

During the ceremony of my being ushered in as a deacon, all kinds of thoughts were racing through my head - mainly, the responsibilities that come with being a deacon. As it is written in 1 Timothy Chapter 3, verses 1-13: This is a true saying, if a man desire the office of a bishop, he desireth a good work.

A bishop then must be blameless, the husband of one wife, vigilant, sober, of good behavior, given to hospitality, apt to teach; not given to wine, no stricker, not greedy of filthy lucre; but patient, not a brawler, not covetous; one that ruleth well his own house, having his children in subjection with all gravity; (for if a man know not how to rule his own house, how shall he take care of the church of God?) not a novice, lest being lifted up with pride he fall into the condemnation of the devil. Moreover, he must have a good report of them which are without; lest he fall into reproach and the snare of the devil. Likewise, must the deacons be grave, not double-tongued, not given to much wine, not greedy of filthy lucre; holding the mystery of the faith in a pure conscience. And let these also first be proved; then let them use the office of a deacon, being found blameless, even so must their wifes be grave, nor slanderers, sober, faithful in all things. Let the deacons be the husbands of one wife, ruling their children and their own houses well. For they that have used the office of a deacon well purchase to themselves a good degree, and great boldness in the faith which is in Christ Jesus.

After having the word of God racing all through my head, I was feeling very doubtful if I could represent the body of Christ Jesus in that capacity. I guess my faith had not grown like I thought; however, I ignored my inner thoughts and went through with the ceremony.

For the next few years I was being used by the Lord in a mighty way. I found myself continuing to witness to the lost and being a loving husband and father. One thing I had truly been amazed with during that time and even now, is how God moved upon my heart to write commentaries. Through the power of the Holy Spirit I started coming up with plays and commentaries for Christmas, Easter, Children's Day and black history programs the church was having each year.

In this book I am going to share with you the readers the most powerful (I personally feel) messages the Lord laid upon my heart to write during the time I first became a deacon. I personally feel these messages will encourage many men, women, and especially children to allow God to direct their hearts with all diligence. I desire so much that many around the world would try the goodness of the Lord. As it is written in Psalms 34, verse 8: 'O taste and see that the Lord is good: Blessed is the man that trusteth in him. Desire in your hearts to trust in the goodness of the Lord, to desire to have an intimate loving relationship with the living Lord Jesus Christ and rest in his love always'.

CHAPTER THIRTY TWO

I will share with you two plays and one commentary in this portion of the book. Two more commentaries will be shared with you toward the end of the book. First will be a play.

A Christmas Play (2001)

Setting: Three kids sitting on a bench singing jingle bells; then a servant of the Lord comes by and observes the kids singing Christmas carols; the servant being filled with joy in his heart when he see the kids singing is prompted to stop and chat with the kids.

Mister: Hey kids, how are you doing?

Kids 1, 2, & 3: FINE!!!

Kid #1: Hey mister where are you going all dressed up?

Mister: I am going to church to celebrate Christmas.

Kid #2: What does church have to do with Christmas?

Mister: I am happy you asked. May I sit with you and tell you?

Kid #3: My mom told me to never ever talk with strangers.

Mister: Your mom told you right; however, I am going to give you each a gift and something to give your parents to read. It is called a tract.

Kid#3: Mister, you seem to be a very nice man. It is OK for you to sit with us for a bit.

Mister: Why thank you very much. Before I give you the gifts and tracts, I must answer the little fellow's question.

Kid #2: Yea mister, what does church have to do with Christmas?

Mister: Well kids, personally I go to church to worship Jesus Christ who is the head of the church.

Kid #1: Head of the church? What do you mean?

Mister: What I mean is that, Jesus is the leader, you know, like the captain of the ship, and one day I hope he will be the captain of your life. Now, I am going to church to sing songs of praise like you were doing when you were singing jingle bells. Also, I am going to pray and to give thanks to God for his free gift to the whole world in the person of his dear son Jesus Christ.

Kid #3: Why would God give his son to the whole world as a free gift?

Mister: That is another very good question. God gave his only begotten son to the world because #1 Love, #2 Sin and #3 Eternal Life.

Kid #2: What is sin?

Mister: Another good question. You are very bright and smart kids. Well, sin is doing things that break God's law. For instance: Stealing, lying to your parents or anyone else you talk to, hating other people, fighting and so on.

Kid #1: Hey Mister, you said something about love and eternal life – tell us about that.

Mister: My pleasure. Now, I am going to give it to you like it was given to me. I am going to tell you what is in the bible.

Kid #3: What is the bible?

Mister: The word bible means book of books. There are 66 books in the bible, 39 in the Old Testament and 27 in the New

Testament. Also, the bible is God's Holy word to mankind. The word holy means divine. God's word is very precious.

Kid #1: Now about love and eternal life.

Mister: Oh yes, as it is written, '…for God so loved the world that he gave his only begotten son that whosoever believeth in him should not perish but have everlasting life. Moreover, he that loveth not knoweth not God; for God is love'. Now it is also written, '…for the wages of sin is death; but the gift of God is eternal life through Jesus Christ our Lord'.

Kid #2: You said something about wages and death.

Mister: When the world began, we human beings fell from God's grace because of our disobedience. It is like when your parents go to work they earn a paycheck and so by our disobedience we earn death spiritually. We are all spiritually dead when we are born into this world. As it is written, '…Wherefore, as by one man sin (Adam) entered into the world, and death by sin; and so death passed upon all men, for that all have sinned…'

Kid #1: He Mister, you mean when everybody is born they or all of us are spiritually dead?

Mister: That is right.

Kid #3: What is a spirit?

Kid #1 & 2: GOOD QUESTION!!!!

Mister: Well, your spirit is your inner most being, your soul if you will. So basically, what I am saying is this: Mankind was in such a lost state spiritually, God sent down to this earth his son to die for all of our sins that we might have eternal life. In other words, when we die physically our soul goes up to heaven to forever be with the Lord. God's greatest gift of all to mankind, his dear son, Jesus Christ. So, at Christmas time we celebrate the birth of God's son Jesus Christ, born in a stable, laid in a manger. Jesus Christ is the reason for the season.

Kid #1: So all of this time I have always thought that Christmas was just for us kids and school vacations.

Kid #2: I always wondered why I saw little play people gathered around a baby in a basket in the front yard of peoples houses.

Kid #3: My parents never told me about this. They fooled me all these years. I wonder why?

Mister: I really do not think that your parents were trying to fool you. Some parents just do not know. Some parents just wait until their kids get a little older. They want their kids to enjoy Christmas very much because they love them very much in their own way and sad to say some parents do not believe in God at all. One other thing I want to share with you is this: Never let anyone tell you there is not a God because there is!

Kid #1: What do we do if someone tries to?

Mister: Tell them to look at the stars, sun, moon, water and how well the human body is put together. There is no way humanly possible that any man or thing could have created what I have just mentioned to you but God almighty himself. As it is written in the word of God, the bible, '...for by him were all things created, that are in heaven, and that are in earth, visible and invisible, whether they be thrones, or dominions, or principalities, or powers': all things were created by Him and for Him. Well, it is time for me to get to church. Here are your gifts and tracts. Do not forget to give the tracts to your parents and tell them that you want to learn more about Jesus.

Kid #3: Hey mister, are you going to be late?

Mister: No, not really. The church I go to, has a late start sometimes. Besides, it was a great joy for me to spend time with you all, and I must say that you kids have truly brought great joy to my heart this day.

Kid #2: Hey Mister, thank you for the gifts and for talking with us.

Mister: You are very welcome.

Kid #1: Hey mister, wait.

(as the kids huddled among themselves, they suddenly turned and shouted)

Kids #1, 2 & 3: JESUS IS THE REASON FOR THE SEASON!!!

Mister: Amen!!!

Now the Second Play

Easter Play 2002

Setting: A panhandler is sitting on a bench across the street from a church on Easter morning begging for money. Suddenly, a servant of the church that sits across the street walks up to the panhandler and starts witnessing to him.

Beggar: Sir, do you have a dollar so I can get something to eat?

Servant: Sure, but before I give you this dollar, I would like to give you some spiritual food. This setting reminds me of a short story in the word of God about a lame man laid in the temple gate daily begging for alms when suddenly, two disciples of Jesus Christ came past. When the man asks for alms, Peter fixed his eyes on the lame man and John said, 'Look on us'. The man looked on them expecting to receive some money. Peter suddenly said, 'Silver and Gold have I none; but such as I have give I thee: in the name of Jesus Christ of Nazareth, rise up and walk.' Peter took the man by the right hand and lifted him up; and immediately his feet and ankle bones received strength. The man leaped up and walked into the temple and started leaping in the air praising God.

The man was full of joy and happiness for the blessing God had laid upon him, and I personally would like to see you filled with that same joy and happiness praising God for it on this Easter morn.

Beggar: Well, I do not think that is going to happen simply because I do not think there is a God. Especially, when I see what is going on around me and all the turmoil I have been through in my life. Also, when I come here asking for money, the people I see are all dressed up going to church. Most of them turn their nose up at me like I am some sort of germ.

Servant: My brother, I sympathize with you concerning this evil world we live in and the selfishness and wickedness that is in the hearts of so many men, women and children that we come in contact with every day. I am very sad to say that every one that puts on a suit and gets all dressed up for church is not what they appear to be on an outward appearance. The bottom line is that their hearts have not been transformed.

Beggar: Transformed, how can a person's heart be transformed? Please explain that to me like I am a four year old.

Servant: My pleasure. First of all, as it is written in God's word, the heart is deceitful above all things, and desperately wicked: who can know it. You see my brother no one knows the depth of evil that is in us. So, it is very important for us all to come to realize it and desire to do something about it. When we are born it is in our nature to hurt others, to do things that are evil. God has provided a way of escape of living an evil, wicked, and defeated life, in the person of his dear son Jesus Christ. Yes, Jesus Christ can and has transformed many hearts.

Beggar: You said something about nature, that it is in our nature to be evil. Why is that?

Servant: As it is written, 'Wherefore, as by one man's sin (Adam) entered into the world, and death by sin; and so death passed upon all men, for that all have sinned: my brother when Adam disobeyed God in the Garden of Eden, he took on a sin nature and so his sin nature passes onto every one that is born into this world.

Beggar: So, what you are saying, we have to suffer for the sin Adam committed. Somehow, that just does not seem fair.

Servant: It is not a point of being fair, because God is a God of love. The entire human race began with Adam and we fall under his blood line. That is the way it is.

Beggar: You said God is a God of love.

Servant: That is right, my brother.

Beggar: Why does God allow so much pain and suffering; for example, me not ever seeing my mother and father, black people being oppressed by white people with slavery, hatred between the races, invasion of war like Pearl Harbor, Vietnam, Hitler ordering the death of thousands of Jews and terrorist attacks like September 11th? Thousands upon thousands of lives lost for what? What is the purpose of all the suffering I have just mentioned to you? If you can explain this to me, I might just believe that there is a God and that God is in fact a God of love.

Servant: First my dear brother, the God that created the heavens and the earth, fowls of the air, fish in the sea, creeping things, animals, water, moon, sun and yes man. God once said in his holy word that He saw the wickedness of man was great in the earth, and that every imagination of the thoughts of his heart was only continually evil. And, it repented the Lord that he had made man on the earth, and it grieved Him at His heart. And the Lord said, I will destroy man whom I have created from the face of the earth; both man and beast, and the creeping things, and the fowls of the air; for it repenteth me that I have made them. In other words God was sorry that he had made man.

God is not a dictator and the human race is not under dictatorship. The human race has the freedom of choice, as it is written, there are none righteous, no, not one; there are none that understandeth, there are none that seeketh after God. They are all gone out of the way, they are together become unprofitable; there are none that doeth good, no, not one. Their throat is an open sepulcher; (meaning grave) with their tongues they have used deceit; the poison of asps (meaning snakes) is under their lips: whose mouth is full of cursing and bitterness: their feet are swift to shed blood: destruction and misery are in their ways: and the way of peace have they not known: there is no fear of God before their eyes. You see my brother, man is very evil. God allows certain things to happen in a person's life to draw that person unto himself. I personally feel that is why you never have seen your mother and father. Moreover, you see how the world has turned away from God; for example, taking prayer out of schools; ministers bringing together men with men in marriage and women with women, instead of teaching abstinence, we are passing out free condoms; and taking Jesus Christ out of Christmas. Also today, when we Christians celebrate Easter, we celebrate the resurrection of our Lord and savior Jesus Christ. Man being evil and paganistic, came up Easter bunnies, jelly beans and Easter egg hunts to take the focus off of the true purpose why we celebrate Easter. You ask why we have so much pain and suffering in the world today and in the past. As it is written, I the Lord search the heart. I try the reins (meaning test the emotions), even to give (meaning repay), every man according to his ways, and according to the fruit of his doings.

Beggar: You have said so much, I am beginning to see why we have so much evil in the world. That old cliché comes to mind that says you reap what you sow. God allows us all to reap the consequences of the choices we make or the fruit we bare.

Servant: You are absolutely correct.

Beggar: I notice that you call me brother a lot. Do you really feel I am your brother and also tell me what Easter is really all about?

Servant: Well, my previous brother, as it is written: God said, Let us make man in our image, after our likeness: moreover, God created man in his own image, in the image of God created he him; male and female created he them. That right there my dear brother makes us brothers. We are all brothers and sisters in this evil world we live in. The only difference is that some are saved and 'Many' are lost.

Beggar: What do you mean lost?

Servant: When we are born into this world, we are spiritually lost or dead, eternally separated from God because of Adam's sin or disobedience; as it is written, for the wages of sin is death; but the gift of God is eternal life through Jesus Christ our Lord.

Now like I stated earlier God is a God of love, as it is written: for God so loved the world that he gave his only begotten son, that whosoever believeth in Him should not parish, but hath everlasting life. In order to be saved my brother, you must put your trust in God's dear son Jesus Christ. As it is written, but as many has received Him, to them gave he the power to become the sons of God, even to them that believe on His name. Moreover, for God sent not his son into the world to condemn the world; but that the world through Him might be saved.

Beggar: You have truly persuaded me to be saved. I want to give my life to Jesus. I want to know the joy and happiness that the lame man had when you first started talking with me.

Servant: That is just wonderful. Le me briefly share with you about Easter. We celebrate the death, burial and resurrection of Jesus Christ. Jesus came upon this earth and died for the sins of the whole world, was buried and raised on the third day. By Jesus being raised on the third day, He conquered spiritual death. When we put our trust in Jesus, we are baptized into the body of Christ through the power of the Holy Spirit. As it is written: we are baptized into his death; that like as Christ was raised up from the dead by the glory of the Father; even so we also should walk in newness of life. Moreover, for if we have been planted together in the likeness of His death, we shall be also in the likeness of His resurrection. That is what Easter is all about my brother if we are in Christ. We should walk in newness of life due to the gospel, the death, burial and resurrection of our Lord and savior Jesus Christ. Are you ready to receive Christ as your savior?

Beggar: Yes, I am.

Servant: First, I am going to thank God for you. Then, I want you to repeat after me.

Beggar: Ok

Servant: Thank you Lord for this brother and given me the privilege to share thy truth with him. May you use him for thy glory. Ok, repeat after me, Dear Lord – I confess that I am a sinner. I believe that Jesus died for my sins – and was buried – and raised on the third day – please Lord Jesus – come into my heart and save me – show me how to live – give me the strength – to faithfully serve you – for the rest of this life you have so freely given me – in Jesus name amen. Welcome to the family my brother. (they hugged)

Beggar: I want to truly thank you for what you have shared with me this day. I will never ever forget it. Matter of fact I would like to praise God in that church across the street.

Servant: Let us go praise him together and after service we will both grab some brunch together. How does that sound to you?

Beggar: Sounds like a sure blessing my brother.

Servant and Beggar: Amen!!!

CHAPTER THIRTY THREE

At the Ark of Love Baptist Church we have many special church services or programs. We have Christmas, Easter, church anniversary and many others. There is one that I really take a special interest in and that is the Children's Day program. I realize that kids all over the world are in fact tomorrow's future. We at the Ark of Love have quite a few kids in our congregation. So, I asked the Lord what would you have me to contribute to this special program for the kids? The Lord laid upon my heart to come up with a commentary that would be a strong encouragement to the kids.

At the Children's Day program the kids do everything from prayer, scripture reading and whatever else that will be performed. The kids do it all. So, the Lord gave me the grace to come up with a commentary that would be easy to understand and also easy for one of the kids to read.

For this particular commentary I had one of the pastor's grandsons to read it. I personally saw in him a great zeal for God in his heart. Even though he read it somewhat fast, he did a wonderful job. Here it is:

Children's Day Commentary 2004

Hi, I come to you this Children's Day celebration to inform you that not only am I a child of the living and true God, but that I am truly tomorrow's future. I want to share with you this day and give you some examples or if you please quote: "Roll models." First my parents and grandparents; they show me a lot of love and encourage me to go to church and learn about God. However, I see that they have their problems which I will gladly keep to myself if I know what is best.

Let me talk about a few sport figures like Michael Jordan: had a gambling problem as well as possibly cheating on his wife. Mr. Charles Barkley: had a very bad attitude and the words he uses at times is just plain bad. OJ Simpson: is possibly a murderer and it is a fact that he did beat and batter his former late wife. Oh and let us not forget about the countless amount of ball players that have been suspended for substance abuse.

Now let us take a look at Hollywood movie stars and how they have been an example to us kids of the future. I would call Hollywood the divorce capital of the world. I personally have heard of more movie stars getting divorced than my peers receiving Jesus Christ as their personal savior. As I see it, I see these married movie actors taking roles in movies, having love affairs or whatever you call it. In my eyes that is adultery or if they are not married, it is called fornication. It is that plain and simple.

Last but not least, our great government. Let us see how our great government has impacted our lives as far as being an example. Every time I turn around it is some kind of scandal going on in our so called great government. It appears that the voting procedures are flawed. We all remember what happened in Florida with President Bush's brother Jeb Bush. They needed a recount and speaking of presidents. Who could forget Mr. Bill Clinton who told a bare faced lie on national television? (I did not have sexual relations with that women) that woman being Monica Lewinski. Yes, the president of the United States of America caught out right committing adultery – some world we live in!

In this world we all live in, it is very hard to find the perfect role model. Personally for me, I have found the perfect role model. Basically, he really found me. That person is none other than the man Christ Jesus.

Jesus Christ has told me in his holy word that he is in fact the bread of life. Moreover, Jesus stated he is the living bread of life that came down from heaven: If any man eat this bread, he shall live forever: and the bread that I will give is my flesh, which I will give for the life of the world. Jesus also told me that, he is the light of the world. As it is written, I am the light of the world: he that followeth me shall not walk in darkness, but shall have the light of life. In continuing, Jesus also says; I am the door: by me if any man enter in, he shall be saved, and shall go in and out, and find pasture.

Moving right along, my Lord and savior stated; I am the good shepherd, I am the resurrection, I am the way, the truth and the life. Moreover, I am the true fine. Basically, Jesus tells me that He is the great I am!! Truly I say to you all that Jesus Christ is not only the savior of the world, but that he is my true example and role model.

As stated in a song by Michael Jackson (man in the mirror), if you want to make the world a better place, take a look at yourself and make that change. That is right my brothers and sisters, change begins with ourselves. We all must be doers of God's word. As it is written; but be ye doers of the word and not hearers only deceiving your own selves. For if any be a hearer of the word, and not a doer, he is like unto a man beholding (which means looking at), his natural face in a glass (which means mirror). For he beholdeth himself, and goeth his way, and straightway (which means immediately), forgetteth what manner man he was.

In closing, I understand that in order for me to be a positive example or role model for everyone I come in contact with mainly my peers, have an impact in this evil world we live in and also make a difference, it begins with me. Take a long look at myself and make a change in my heart.

I must follow and serve the Lord of Lords and King of Kings: the man Christ Jesus every day with all of my heart, mind, body and soul. This is what I want and must do because I love the Lord and I am truly tomorrow's future. Those who have ears let him hear. Thank you and Amen. That was such a wonderful service because the kids received a strong encouragement with what was done and said throughout the entire service. Moreover, the adults including myself received quite a blessing and an encouragement from all that was done and said by the kids. As I see it, kids are in fact tomorrow's future.

Chapter Thirty Four

At this time things were going quite well in this life God has so freely given me. My security job was going great with my promotion and all; however, some of the guys were jealous about me getting the promotion.

The young lady that worked part-time was informing me that they were expressing their feelings toward me to her. I was informed that they were putting out rumors about me having affairs with other women mainly the nurses in the nursing home – which I was not – at that time anyway. In spite of all that was going on with my coworkers, I continued to go about my job in a very professional manner.

My co-workers did not like the fact of me driving on the sites checking on them. In fact I was catching quite a few of them asleep or away from the site. Unfortunately, I had a few co-workers fired. It was my job and I was very happy that most of my co-workers understood.

As far as my life was concerned, after several years of going to church, working almost every day, being a loving husband and father to my kids, things were beginning to unravel between my wife and I. My wife and I started arguing over small things, such as her hair being in the food. My wife's hair was very long and straight as she was from Panama – a very pretty Spanish lady. We also argued about the bills and my household cleaning habits. I like the house being very neat and clean. Things were beginning to get very ugly especially when it came to correcting or disciplining my son. She would stop me from giving him a beating with my belt. I even reminded her what the word of God says about disciplining your children. As it is written; Proverbs Chapter 13, verse 24: He that spareth his rod hateth his son: but he that loveth him chasteneth him bedtimes – (which means early).

Before I would correct my son I would always explain to him that verse and share with him how much I loved him and how much it hurt me to correct him in the manner of a beating with my belt.

After church my wife and I argued about what the pastor preached about. She would start yelling at me. This arguing was happening on a more frequent basis. I mean as soon as we were on our way home from church; it was almost as though she was picking an argument on purpose. What made it so bad; she would do this right in front of the kids.

My feelings for my wife were turning toward the worse and it was nothing I could do about it. I even tried having family bible studies; things were getting a little better up until the topic was prayer. My wife informed me that we do not need to pray. Her reasoning was if God is God, he already knew what we needed and that God knows everything.

I gracefully explained to her what the word of God says concerning prayer. I will share just one verse from the bible concerning prayer. As it is written in Colossians Chapter 1, verse 9: For this cause we also, since the day we heard it, do not cease to pray for you, and to desire that ye might be filled with the knowledge of his will in all wisdom and spiritual understanding.

There are many other verses in the word of God that encourages us to pray on a regular basis. I ask her why do we have the Lord's Prayer in the bible? She gave me no reply to that – just a lot of yelling.

As the weeks went on things were getting much worse. My wife and I had stopped having sex with one another because at this point I had no desire what-so-ever. My sweet loving wife at one time resorted to calling me names, putting me down by telling me that I think that I was better than everybody else; I was a know-it-all and that I do not know how to raise my kids. She even threw up in my face about how I was a stupid drug addict for no apparent reason. As quickly as I could, I called my pastor and explained to him what was going on and he suggested going to marriage counseling. I agreed, but my wife did not want to. I believe that she was just tired to being with me; however, she never stated it to me that she was. One night we were all gathered at the dinner table getting ready for dinner. She brought the dinner out onto the table. We were having hamburger helper. I will never forget that night as it truly was a nightmare. Her hair was mixed in throughout the entire dish. I explained to her that hair carried more germs than any other part of the human body. Her reply to that was she thought it was very funny. At that time I was almost to the point of tears and had made up my mind that I had enough of putting up with her foolishness. I felt within my heart that the relationship was over.

CHAPTER THIRTY FIVE

After that incident at the dinner table I stormed out of the house and got into my car. I just drove away and back into the life God had freed me from several years ago. As I was driving that night, I was saying to myself why is God allowing this to happen to me? Suddenly, I thought to myself, maybe God is just making me a stronger Christian. I really did not know but one thing. I was sick and tired of my wife treating me the way she was and I wanted out in the worse way.

That night I went back to the house and took about half the money I had in the lock box and promptly left back out of the house to begin a life that I truly regret to this day. As I left the house the thoughts that were racing through my mind were that I was about to allow the devil to ruin my life completely and also what the word of God says about how the devil is a roaring lion seeking whom he may devour. Moreover, as it is written, Ephesians, Chapter 6, verses 10-12: Finally, my brethren, be strong in the Lord, and in the power of his might. Put on the whole armour of God, that ye may be able to stand against the wiles of the devil. For we wrestle not against flesh and blood, but against principalities, against powers, against the rulers of the darkness of this world, against spiritual wickedness in high places. As all of those thoughts were racing through my mind, I was beginning to feel sorry for myself and thought I deserved better. I wanted to be happy and wanted a woman to really love me faithfully. On my way to D.C. I continued thinking to myself how I was not strong enough to win this battle with the devil. I really hated the thought of being defeated by the devil. There is a saying that the truth hurts.

That night I really did not care or to be more honest I will say that I did not allow myself to care because in reality I really did. My dear beloved brothers and sisters that night I became a backsliding sinner.

I went to D.C. and started a very carnal lifestyle once again destroying what the Lord Jesus Christ had given me the will to build up which was a Christian home, Christ loving friendships, a good job and last but not least an intimate loving relationship with my Lord and saviour Jesus Christ. I had allowed the behavior of someone else to dictate my emotions and behavior. Now that night I had come back home very late. It was about 4:00 or 5:00 a.m. in the morning. My wife and I did not say a word to each other. I managed to work for about another week.

When I found myself using crack cocaine on the job, I knew it was time for me to quit. So, I quit my job and found myself back on the streets being a servant of the devil. For the next year or so, I was in and out of shelters, still using crack and living like the wretched sinner I was. I had come to the point where I was just plain tired of living this lifestyle, so I thought. I checked into a detox program and from there I promptly checked into another drug program.

CHAPTER THIRTY SIX

The name of this drug program was New Beginnings located in Chantilly, Virginia. Basically, it was no different than the others I had successfully completed. However, this program truly did succeed in getting me to get in touch with some deep rooted feelings I did not think I had. Once again, I was going to AA and NA meetings, listening to various stories how drugs and alcohol ruined people's lives. The one thing I was not happy with was the way others get very uncomfortable when God is mentioned or when I and a very few others share about the role that God played in our lives. Life was showing me that there is a higher percentage of the human race that does not wish to hear anything about God than those that do. For a very long time I often wondered why until God revealed the answer to me from his holy and precious word. As it is written in St. John Chapter 3, verse 19: and this is the condemnation, (which means judgment), that light is come into the world, and men loved darkness rather than light, because their deeds were evil.

After completing three months of the drug program, I stayed at a men's home for recovering addicts. It was a pretty nice place. The house was very big, located not too far from the drug treatment center I had just left. I really did not allow myself to get attached to any of the other addicts staying there because I was just focusing on what I must do to get my life back in order.

During my stay at the men's home, I promptly found a job at an Exxon gas station as a cashier. I was going to work every day or when scheduled to work and I had to also attend NA and AA meetings every day. As I was attending these meetings, I was not getting very much out of them because one, I really did not want to be at those meetings and two, I found myself deep in thought about my daughter which at this time was living in Fredericksburg, Virginia with her aunt, thinking about my son, pastor of the Ark of Love, and the assistant Chaplin of the Salvation Army, which at this time had passed away. One thing that the assistant Chaplin told me that has always and even to this day has had a deep affect on my heart, he said to me on several occasions that I, Victor Bradford, was voted most likely to succeed. At this point and time the only thing I was succeeding in was destroying and making a mess of this life God has so freely given me and that was a fact my dear brothers and sisters.

As I continued to stay at the men's home, I was saving my money until I had enough to buy a car. After about two months or so I finally had enough money to buy a car. So, I shot over to Woodbridge, Virginia where you could buy a car for a very reasonable price. I purchased a dark blue Buick Century and I truly loved that car. That was the first car I bought that gave me very little problems. After buying the car, I stayed at the men's home for about another month. Before you know it I was off to the races again.

CHAPTER THIRTY SEVEN

This time around I found myself doing things I thought I was incapable of. I had come to the realization that I was on a mission to kill myself but was unable to do anything about it. I found myself back in D.C. hunting down women that used crack, having them perform oral sex on me. When the money ran out I found myself driving up and down the Washington D.C. streets asking people if they needed rides. People who do that are called gypsy cab drivers. The money was great; however, it is illegal.

Then I started running into male drug users. Some of them were showing me the ropes as far as making money with a car. One guy told me about the Greyhound Bus Station in Northwest D.C. Now that was a serious money maker there. Then I met male and female crack users that were called boosters. Boosters are people who go into department stores, grocery stores or whatever kind of store and steal items, then sell them for money or drugs. I found myself getting a percentage of their take because I was giving some of them rides to the stores.

Then I found myself being hooked up with this one girl because I did not like associating with a lot of people. She was really good at her craft, meaning stealing. I tried to encourage her to save the money and let it build up, but she could not wait to get high again. I mean as soon as she got the money in her hand she was ready to smoke again. I had to cut her back in a hurry, so I just started going back down to the Greyhound Bus Station. It was illegal to give people rides unless you had a chauffeur's license to do so. So, I was very leery of doing that because if the police caught you, they would impound your car and possibly send you to jail.

At this point and time in my life, I was getting very little sleep. I was very paranoid. I personally felt that my wife, pastor and others I knew were following me when I was driving around giving people rides. However, I did not let that stop me from doing what I was doing. Next, I found myself in front of grocery stores giving people rides with their groceries. That was really a money maker too. When I was tired I drove my car to a nice peaceful place and went straight to sleep; then got up to do the same thing all over again. I was not bathing or brushing my teeth and I was beginning to look horrible. I do mean HORRIBLE. And you know what, at that time I really did not care. I was hanging out at crack houses, driving drug dealers around so I could get crack and loaning my car out to get crack.

My life was really getting worse and worse and I knew a time was coming when I would have to pay for it all. Throughout this evil living I was mixed up in, I had met a guy who was always at his van on a street corner selling and buying stolen items, from cameras, films, video tapes and anything that had any value to it. So, I took it upon myself to go into a Rite Aid Pharmacy, grabbed a little red basket and filled it up with cameras and film. Then, instead of going straight out the front door, being the nervous thief I was, I took the liberty to walk all the way around the store and in the process I walked directly past the manager's office where she and others were standing having a conversation. To my surprise they saw what I had in the basket. When I finally arrived at the front entrance and exit door I took off running. My car was right in front of the door. I felt that I could not go to my car because I felt them behind me and sure enough they were chasing after me. When I made it across the street I was at Linsey's Cadillac parking lot. I promptly put the basket between some cars that was in the parking lot and continued to run for my life but I wanted to stay close enough so I could get to my car.

The store employees were still chasing me. In my mind I was thinking that they were not supposed to be chasing me because when you work in a retail store they train you to never ever chase after a would-be thief or robber. Well, I guess they through out the rule book as during this chase I somehow made it to the back of the Rite Aid store where there was a tall wooden fence. As I was attempting to climb the fence one of the employees ran up on me and grabbed my legs and pushed them over the fence – almost as if I was doing a cartwheel over the tall wooden fence. Yes, my beloved brothers and sisters, yours truly landed on his right hip. I had fallen on the solid cement and later that employee lied about touching me because I heard the manager ask him if he touched me. I was truly in too much pain to say anything.

CHAPTER THIRTY EIGHT

Well, my brothers and sisters, I found myself laid up in Alexandria Hospital. The same hospital I had worked at for about seven years. The Rite Aid store where I was at was close to Bradlee Shopping Center in which was very close to the hospital. You would think that this ordeal would have brought an end to my drug use, not hardly. As I laid in that emergency room a scripture came to mind - one that I refused to think about during my run of evil. As it is written in Hebrews Chapter 12, verses 5-6: And ye have forgotten the exhortation which speaketh unto you as unto children, my son, despise not thou the chastening of the Lord, nor faint when thou art rebuked of him: for whom the Lord loveth he chasteneth (meaning corrects) and scourgeth every son whom he receiveth. Yes, my beloveds, I knew the time was coming because I knew within my heart that the Lord was fed up with me and has had enough of my foolish and evil wicked ways. The same way I was fed up with my wife's foolishness. There is an old saying that goes like this: What goes around will eventually come around. It had sure enough come around to me because I was in so much pain, it was truly unbearable.

The police were in the ER with me. The last thing I remember being in the ER was hearing a policeman saying to another policeman that they did not have to worry about me running because I was busted up pretty good as they were gazing at my x-rays. Finally, I was taken up to my room and when I finally came around, the nurse informed me that a doctor would be in to see me later.

After lying in my hospital bed feeling sorry for myself for a while, the doctor finally came in to see me and informed me of the extent of my injury. The good doctor informed me that my right hip was broken and also my right femur was crushed and if that was not enough he told me as he was leaving out of the room, I would be lucky if I ever was able to walk again.

At that moment my whole world, what was left of it, had truly come crashing down around me. Well, I said to myself, Lord, where do we go from here.

The surgery took place the next day. The doctor told me that the surgery went better than he anticipated. He informed me that he put a prosthesis in my right hip to hold it together and seven long screws to hold my femur together. I was in the hospital for over two months. When the time came for me to leave, I had to act fast in finding a shelter that would accept someone on crutches.

By the grace of God alone I found one in D.C. I truly had a hard time of it. The doctor had told me to be extra careful because of the stitches I had in my hip. I stayed at this shelter in D.C. for a short while because I truly hated it. That was one of the dirtiest shelters I have ever seen and also I had to do too much moving around, going to drug and health meetings. I stayed there just long enough to get my stitches removed. I called an old girlfriend of mine that I had met at one of the drug programs I was in and promptly explained to her my situation.

Chapter Thirty Nine

After about a week from getting my stitches removed, the young lady I called came to pick me up from the shelter to visit her at her home. When you are staying at a shelter, they make it very clear that you have to be back by the curfew they set forth and not a minute later. That night I made it back five minutes after curfew and they did not let me in. They did not care that I was on crutches and was not in the best of health, they just out right said NO.

So my friend took me back to her house in Alexandria, Virginia. She informed me that I could stay at her house until I could find another shelter. After staying with her and her kids for about a month, I finally found a shelter in Manassas, Virginia. The good thing about that shelter was that it was a lot cleaner but they had strict rules about curfew also which I found out about a few weeks down the road. Before that time came I was informed that there was a social service building right around the corner from the shelter. I promptly ambled my way to the social service building on crutches and all and applied for the Section-8 Program and public housing. I also applied for social security disability income. After I had applied for those services, I managed to stay at that shelter for about two weeks. My friend came to visit and sure enough I was late again. So there I was staying with my friend again. Her kids just kept her busy all the time and were always getting in trouble. It was either school or one of her boys getting caught stealing. She had three boys and two girls. The strange thing about this situation was that she and I were not having any sexual intimacy at all, even though I would have loved to.

She was about 5'7", about 135 pounds and she truly had a double d chest size. (Even to this day I still see her from time to time when she needs to borrow some money or something.) I was truly unhappy because I was beginning to miss my son and doing all the fun things that brought so much joy to my heart. After staying there about another month, I grabbed a phone book and looked up the phone number to one of the deacons of the Ark of Love Baptist Church. By the grace of God, I found the number I was looking for. I promptly called him and there was no answer, so I left him a message briefly explaining to him my situation.

He called me at my friend's house later on that night and we talked for about twenty minutes. After it was all said and done, he informed me that it was ok for me to stay with him or until I get my life back in order. I tell you my precious brothers and sisters I was one happy sinner that night. He came to pick me up and took me to my wife's house where I had more clothes. I briefly saw my son and chatted with him for a while then went to Springfield, Virginia where the deacon lived.

At that time I was walking with a limp due to my surgery and was still feeling a lot of pain. The deacon of the church had informed me that his job would be sending him to Alaska for a few months and asked if I would be ok. I told him yes and that I was very happy to have a place to live. I was truly grateful for his loving kindness.

After a few months had past, I had met the deacon's friendly neighbors. There was a family of four with one little girl and boy. The oldest boy was about four and the girl was about two. They started taking me to their church. One of the deacons had bought me a brand new bible and the neighbors had bought me a very nice looking carrying cover with handles for my bible. To this day I am still using the same bible and carrying cover.

God was showing me how much he really loved me in spite of myself. As I continued going to church and getting back into the routine of faithfully serving the Lord with the encouragement of the deacon's neighbor, I still had increasingly more pain in my right hip. I called my doctor and informed him of the pain I was having. He told me to come into his office so he could look at me. After the doctor saw the x-rays he informed me that the prosthesis I had in my right hip had broken in half and also three of the screws had broken in my femur. He told me that I needed to have another operation. I was one unhappy sinner. However, I truly had a lot to be thankful for, that was for sure. My neighbor's wife took me to the hospital the day of the surgery and gave me a very loving hug just before she left the hospital.

Chapter Forty

After the surgery, I found myself in my hospital room and in much pain. The doctor came to my room and informed me that the surgery had taken five and half hours, three hours longer than the first operation. He informed me that it took so long because he had a hard time getting the old screws out that had broken in my femur. He went on to explain to me that there would be some discomfort for a while but that I should heal nicely.

After being in the hospital for about a week, my neighbor came to pick me up. The deacon had called me and told me that he would be in Alaska longer than he anticipated and that he did not know exactly when he would be back home. He also said that he hoped my hip healed properly and that he would be praying for me.

About three months had past and my hip had healed to the point I no longer needed my crutches. However, I still had a hard time sleeping on my right side. Also, the deacon had finally come back home. He was not very happy with me for rearranging the furniture in his house; however, he said that it did look very nice.

As the months past I continued going to church with the deacon and talking with my son and daughter. Things were beginning to look up for me up until I finally received my social security income. I received a retroactive check meaning that I was paid from when I first applied. I never in my life received a check with that amount of money. This was about the first week of January 2000. Having that amount of money in my hand was a serious temptation; however, I did not bother to think along those lines at that time.

The first thing I did was give the deacon some money. Then, I went out to buy myself another car because the Buick Century I bought was towed away from the Rite-Aid Pharmacy parking lot and more than likely was sold. However, I still had to pay taxes on it in order for me to get the necessary stickers for my new car.

After buying my little blue sports car, I could not wait to get to D.C. and start the same evil lifestyle that crippled me physically, mentally and spiritually. When I arrived back home early the next morning I was very ashamed of myself for allowing myself to continue this evil way of living.

I did not tell the deacon what I had done. I informed him that I was with a lady friend. I had resorted to lying to a man of God. I knew that this could not continue but it did for several months. I felt within myself that I was living on borrowed time and that my sin would catch up with me sooner or later. So, I went down on my knees and asked the Lord to give me the power from above to bring an end to this evil lifestyle.

For the next month or so I stayed away from D.C. and that carnal life I was living. The deacon and I were going to church on a regular basis. I was also going to church with my neighbors. I was doing anything to keep my mind occupied with spiritual things. The one thing that I loved so much was listening to Christian broadcasting on the radio. The programs I listened to the most were Through the Bible with Jay Vernon McGee, The Urban Alternative with Dr. Tony Evans, the radio and television ministry of Dr. Charles Stanley and Unshackled.

Those are the main programs I love to listen to; however, there are many others. My favorite radio stations are 95.1 FM WRBS; 105.1 FM WAVA; 1220 AM WFAX; and 107.7 FM family radio. I am very thankful for these programs on the radio as I strongly feel that God has used these programs to encourage and strengthen many sinners around the world such as myself to faithfully serve the living Lord with all of our hearts, minds, bodies and souls.

After about two months or so had gone by, the deacon told me that his job would be sending him to Roanoke, Virginia Monday through Friday, and that he would come back home every weekend. At that time, that was a serious temptation for me. My flesh would say I have the house to myself for the whole week. When the deacon would leave Sunday nights on his way to Roanoke, Virginia, I promptly would start back into this evil lifestyle from time to time. I was beginning to hate myself for continuing to turn my back on the God who has shown his love to me throughout this life that he has so freely given me.

When the money ran out I even resorted to pawning items that belonged to the deacon such as his flat keyboard organ, tools, and TV. After pawning those items for money to buy more crack cocaine, I knew things were beginning to get out of hand again. By the grace of God, I finally received in the mail my Section-8 voucher,

CHAPTER FORTY ONE

I was now able to get my very own place. Just before I moved I explained to the deacon what I had done as far as pawning his items for money to get crack cocaine. I apologized to him for doing this evil to him. He was very forgiving and he also wished me well in my new home. I had managed since then to give him back some of the money I owed him, plus giving him another television.

It was the beginning of 2002 when I moved into my new home. I did not have any furniture at first. The Lord laid upon my heart to call around to different churches to see if I could get some furniture for my condo. The Salvation Army gave me a voucher for over $500 and another church had given me a lovely big red oak bed and dresser that I still have to this very day.

In spite of myself God continues to bless me beyond comprehension. Almost everything I have in my condo today was given to me except for most of the pictures I have on my walls and a few lamps. Not too long after that I received another voucher from the Salvation Army to get furniture for my living room which was a blessing from the Lord.

I settled into my home and promptly called my daughter who was now living with her mother in Woodbridge, Virginia. I called my son and told him where I was living and also called the pastor of the Ark of Love to inform him of the good news.

After being in my place a few months, I focused on building a relationship with my daughter because of my previous evil living I did not spend much time with her during her younger years. The Lord gave me the grace to plant seeds in her heart meaning his holy and precious word. To this day I am very thankful that the Lord has given me the privilege to share his word with her, and as I write this book she is faithfully serving the Lord and I do mean faithfully. My daughter has been a big encouragement to me in the last few years of this life God has so freely given me. As it is written in Isaiah Chapter 55, verses 10-11: For as the rain cometh down, and the snow from heaven, and returneth not thither, but watereth the earth, and maketh it bring forth and bud, that it may give seed to the sower, and bread to the eater: so shall my word be that goeth forth out of my mouth: it shall not return unto me void, but it shall accomplish that which I please, and it shall prosper in the thing whereto I sent it. The word of God is performing a good work in the life of my daughter and I am truly grateful for the power of the living and true God.

During this process of me building a relationship with my kids, I started working at Carquest Auto Parts as a driver. It was a very nice job. I was basically my own boss, just delivering auto parts. At this time I was going to church but not as regularly as I should have and it cost me because I began to do things that were unbecoming of a servant of the living God.

CHAPTER FORTY TWO

Now the time had come when I started going out and paying women to perform oral sex on me and before I knew it I was using crack again. I was staying away from the house two and three days at a time, hanging out at the Greyhound Bus Station again, and driving up and down the streets of D.C. giving people rides for money so I could support my crack habit. I was one pitiful individual – I really was. The time had come for me to renew my Section-8 voucher and I was given the opportunity to get a two bedroom condo which cost $1,000 a month. All I had to pay was $244 a month and the government paid the rest. This two bedroom condo which was called Pinewood South Condominiums was in the same complex where I was living.

I had to stop working at the auto parts store due to me getting two speeding tickets while making deliveries. It really did not bother me that much because I was still getting a disability check every third of each month.

After settling into my new home, I met two guys who were cousins, who were also crack dealers that had just started hanging out in the same neighborhood I was living. I also met a woman and her husband who also sold crack in the next complex down from mine. To get more money in my hands, I promptly rented out my second bedroom. First, I rented it to a white gentleman that was referred to me by someone from a church that had read my ad that I put in the newspaper. He turned out to be a drunk. I allowed him to stay with me for about six months. Then I put the ad back in the papers. Next, I allowed a woman to move in who was referred to me from someone from Social Services.

During this time I was having roommates, I was still using crack and allowing different drug dealers to come into my house to sell me crack cocaine. I was not calling my kids and was surely not going to church at all. My life was taking a turn for the worst. You would think the injury to my right hip would have been my wake-up call; it was not. By having roommates, I did not have to go to D.C. to give people rides for money; moreover, I did not have to go to D.C. to buy crack because it was right at my doorstep.

As far as this woman was concerned she was somewhat attractive; however, I was not going to pursue an intimate relationship with her because of the possibility of her asking for her rent to be cut in half or something. I was charging her $400 a month which I thought was very reasonable compared to what I saw others charging for rooms to rent. The lady I was renting this room to appeared to be a very nice lady at first. About a month went by and she started acting very strange, talking to herself, accusing the guys I had over the house of trying to scare her when she came out of the bathroom and other things that I will not mention in this book.

Due to a very bad habit I had picked up (ordering porno movies) when I moved into my first condo and continued when I moved to the two bedroom condo, my combined cable bill was over $1,000. So naturally, my cable was cut off from lack of payment. I took the liberty to use my roommate's name to get the cable cut back on. The only thing I was paying for was rent and household needs. I did not care how bad my addition was; but I never ever had a dirty home and I mean that from my heart.

I also bought food from time to time and was also able to get food from churches and other places that help families with food.

So food was never an issue. The phone bill was always paid as I felt that my phone was a very vital, and the last of my money went to the crack dealers. After four months past, she wanted to move out because she was now able to get her own place through the Section-8 program. I allowed her to move out and she asked me to give her a good reference to the apartment where she was moving. Well, she found out about me using her name to get cable before I had a chance to change it because she started getting her mail sent to the Post Office. After she found out she informed me that she was going to get a lawyer and have me jailed for using her name to get cable. I promptly wrote her a letter of apology; however, it did no good as she kept the letter to show my guilt. Down the road I would surely pay the price and that my brothers and sisters was the turning point for the rest of this life God had so freely given me. After she moved out I had the nerve to allow one of the cousins that was a crack dealer to move into the second bedroom – what a tremendous mistake! THAT TOO WAS ANOTHER TURNING POINT!!

CHAPTER FORTY THREE

After allowing a crack dealer into my house, things were really taking a turn for the worst and I do mean the WORST! As the months went by, people were coming to the house to buy crack. I was meeting women that used crack that wanted to come into my house and smoke. I allowed guys and women to come in and smoke, so I could get some for myself. On top of that the crack dealer's friends were coming to my house and hanging out - which I hated with a passion.

At one point I was just fed up. I drove to D.C. and bought some crack and just hung out over there. I found myself at a crack dealer's house in D.C. and when my money run out, I rented my car out for crack to a guy I had never seen before in my life; however, I gave it to him anyway. And of course I have never seen him since. Yes my beloveds, he never brought the car back. I called the deacon that I had lived with in Springfield, Virginia to come pick me up and to take me home. When the deacon came to pick me up, I explained to him what had happened and also asked him for some money. I told him that I owed someone the money, and he promptly gave it to me.

When I finally arrived at home I called the police and told them that my car had been stolen. Then, my roommate the crack dealer had come in, and I promptly bought some crack with the money the deacon had given me. Needless to say at this time, my life was truly out of control and I was wondering to myself will it ever get better? A few months past and the police called to inform me that my car was found.

I called the deacon to see if he could take me to pick up my car and he did. When we reached the location of my car, I tried to start it and of course it would not start. As we looked at it, we noticed that it did not have any antifreeze in the radiator. When we put some in, it finally started and I drove it a good half a mile before it just gave out. So, I just left it on the side of the road and said to myself – another lesson learned – never ever allow anyone else to drive my car. That is if I ever have the opportunity to own another car.

I now had a roommate that was paying his rent with crack. I neglected my responsibilities as a servant of the living Lord, neglected my responsibilities as a father to my kids, no longer had a car, had the potential of being put in jail for cable fraud, and last but not least my home had turned into a crack house. To relieve myself of the pressure I was under, I started working little odd jobs for Labor Ready. Labor Ready is a place where you go in the morning and sit until your name is called to go out and work wherever they send you – from construction to warehouse work and at the end of the day you would get paid.

I did this off and on for several months and in the process I met a young lady in the area I lived. She appeared to be a sweet young lady and we were seeing each other for a while and in the process I told her what was going on in my household. As well as the relationship I desired to have with the Lord and my kids again. She was encouraging me to put the crack dealer out of my house and to stop using crack. I told her that I really do not know how to go about it.

CHAPTER FORTY FOUR

The lady friend that I had just met was very slim built with small breast, was about 5'7", weighed about 130 pounds, wore glasses, and was fairly attractive. She informed me that she used to smoke crack too and that she lived with her sister and kids. They lived in a very big house that was not too far from where I was living. When she informed me that she smoked marijuana, I knew then that I really did not want to get too serious with her.

As I was wondering what to do with the situation I was in, things started to happen. First, my wife had me to sign divorce papers. I received mail concerning the incident with the cable fraud which at that time I did not think too much about it. In other words I did not think I would go to jail for such a thing. On a night I had people over the house smoking crack, the crack dealer and his cousin got into a heated argument about taking sales from each other. They were yelling at the top of their lungs – as if what they were yelling about was legal.

I knew this had to come to an end. After about 20 minutes of this bickering, I was able to calm them both down. They were truly on their way to fist fighting each other. I just looked around, seeing people smoking crack, the cousins about to fight and me being ordered to be in court in a few months for cable fraud. And, the last time I spoke to my lady friend she told me the police were watching my house.

I said to myself I must do something right now because I have had enough. I did that the very next day. I informed the crack dealer that I was being evicted because of complaints from the neighbors of having drug users coming to my house at all hours of the night. I also informed the Section-8 agency of black mold I had on my ceiling and walls in my bedroom, kitchen and dining room. They understood, so within a few days, I moved in with my lady friend I was currently seeing. She and her family had recently just moved into a huge five bedroom house. It was perfect timing because I had just received my disability check and I was able to pay them the $200 they wanted for the month.

I was very happy things happened the way it did. Before you know it I was no longer using crack. I was no longer surrounded by crack users and also had the opportunity to get a fresh start at a new place of residence.

At this time it was the winter of 2004 and the Section-8 agency finally gave me a list of places that I could move to. I found a place just as fast as I could so I could have a peaceful nights sleep. Make no mistake I was truly appreciative of my lady friend and her family allowing me to stay with them until I was able to get my own place. Just before I moved I surely extended my gratitude toward their generosity and moved with great swiftness.

To my surprise I could not find anyone to help me move in my new place except for one person and that was the crack dealer that had lived with me. I promptly informed him that my crack using days were over for good, and I was never more serious because I was sick of it all.

CHAPTER FORTY FIVE

I managed to find another two bedroom condo. The name of the complex was the Villages. The Lord had truly given me the opportunity to start this life all over again. However, the only difference was that I was loaded with so much knowledge from the word of God and I knew that the Lord was going to use that knowledge for his good purpose.

This time around it was going to be different and how you may ask? That is instead of only knowing God's holy word, but just literally acting on the knowledge of God's holy word. Remember what I had stated back in the children's day commentary about what God says in his word about being not just hearers of the word but be ye doers of the word? That is what I am putting into practice these days my beloveds.

After moving into my new home things were going fairly well. The crack dealer dropped over a few times to see if I was staying clean and sober. To his disappointment I was and was giving him some words of wisdom in the process and to this day it has locked hold of his life. God is an awesome God; make no mistake my brothers and sisters.

My son and his mother had started coming to my home to spend time with me and on top of that my daughter had started visiting me. God had given me the opportunity to have a loving relationship with my kids. That has truly brought great joy to my heart. My step-daughter is now married and just had a little baby boy who lives in Kentucky. My daughter is currently continuing her walk with the Lord, being an example of a true child of the living and true God. I am so proud of her for sure. My son is having somewhat of a rough time. He has graduated from high school and started going to a local college part time. However, after getting his driver's license he managed to get a few traffic violations and not helping his mother around the house that she is currently buying in Lorton, Virginia which is minutes from where I now live. Things are beginning to get better in his life. We all must be patient with our kids the same way God is patient with us wretched sinners. I truly can relate to Paul when he said as he was moved by the Holy Spirit, as it is written in 1 Timothy Chapter 1, verse 15: This is a faithful saying, and worthy of all acceptation, that Christ Jesus came into the world to save sinners; of whom I am chief. Yes, my beloveds, I truly feel that I am a chief sinner, especially as I look back on how I was living in the presence of the Lord.

I was very busy reestablishing relationships with the Lord Jesus Christ, my kids, and church members. I took the liberty to get a job as a Security Officer working 9:00 PM to 5:00 AM at a high rise apartment complex which was fairly close to where I lived. Things were really beginning to look up for me. I was also building a relationship with my landlords whom are FBI agents. I must say that was a huge incentive for me to stay out of trouble. I said to myself the Lord knows exactly what he is doing at all times. As far as my lady friend that I had met a few months back, we were not seeing much of each other because basically, I really did not have any desire to be with her at all.

Chapter Forty Six

One night as I was going to work I met a very nice lady on the bus. She was about five foot tall with hazel eyes and the biggest breast I have ever seen a woman posses. I mean she would put Dolly Parton's breast to shame. She informed me that she was from the Virgin Island. She had the prettiest skin which was the shade of caramel. I was very happy I met her because I had someone to talk to during the hours I was at work. Working security at night can be somewhat boring. The only thing I had to do was to patrol the parking lot, lobby and basement areas. The lady friend (which I will call her Shorty) and I had formed a relationship. She informed me that she was a supervisor at the Wal-Mart department store.

Since I was no longer spending all my money on crack cocaine, I took the liberty to rent a car on a monthly basis for a very low price. The name of the place was called Bargain Rental Car.

Shorty and I were building a relationship. I finally broke down and told her of the situation with the court date I had coming very soon; however, I did not tell her about my bout with crack cocaine. In the short period that we were seeing each other, my feelings for her were growing. She treated me with so much kindness that I was not used to. She was always buying me dinner, just basically buying me whatever I wanted. She was always putting gas in my rental car and loving me constantly – I mean every chance she had.

Even though she was showering me with so much loving kindness, deep down in my heart I knew that I was wrong by having sex with her because I do know how God feels about a man and woman having sex out of the bonds of marriage. The word of God calls it fornicating, and I knew a price would have to be paid for my carnal living. For it is written in Job Chapter 4, verse 8: Even as I have seen, they that plow iniquity, (which means sin) and sow wickedness, reap the same. Moreover, as it is also written in Galatians Chapter 5, verses 16-25: This I say then, walk in the spirit, and ye shall not fulfill the lust of the flesh. For the flesh lusteth against the spirit and the spirit against the flesh: and these are contrary to one to the other: so that ye cannot do the things that ye would. But if ye be led of the spirit, ye are not under the law. Now the works of the flesh are manifest (which means made known) which are these; adultery, fornication, uncleanness, lasciviousness, idolatry, witchcraft, hatred, variance, emulations, wrath, strife, seditions, heresies, envyings, murders, drunkenness, revellings, and such like: of the which I tell you before, as I have told you in times past, that they which do such things shall not inherit the kingdom of God. But the fruit of the spirit is love, joy, peace, longsuffering, gentleness, goodness, faith, meekness, temperance: against such there is no law. And they that are Christ's have crucified the flesh with the affections and lusts. If we live in spirit, let us also walk in the spirit.

Yes, my beloveds, God make it plain and clear how he feels about wicked, carnal and very evil living. At this time of my life, it was getting to the point that I was unable to enjoy pleasing the flesh. The Holy Spirit that was dwelling in me was convicting me of my carnal ways and that was a fact and even to this very day.

Now concerning the relationship that Shorty and I were having - I promptly sat her down and explained to her the mixed emotions I was having concerning our sexual lifestyle. Her response was that God understands our weaknesses and that we are not perfect. I told her that is so true; however, the God I serve is a jealous God and as it is written in Exodus Chapter 20, verses 4-6: Thou shalt not make unto thee any graven image, or any likeness of any thing that is in the heaven above, or that is in the earth beneath, or that is in the water under the earth: Thou shalt not bow down (which means worship) thyself to them, nor serve them, for I the Lord thy God am a jealous God, visiting the iniquity of the fathers upon the children unto the third and fourth generation of them that hate me; and shewing mercy unto thousands of them that love me and keep my commandments.

After sharing this with her, we continued to see each other; however, it appeared that she was not very happy with me because we were not having sex as much as she would have liked. She did continue to be a dear loving friend.

CHAPTER FORTY SEVEN

Well my beloveds it was May 9, 2005 – time had finally come for me to go to court for cable fraud. For some reason I had a very uneasy feeling about this simply because my court appointed lawyer never called me to discuss the case. The first time I saw him was the day of the trial. I asked him if there was a chance of me being locked up for this charge and he promptly told me that there was a fifty-fifty chance of me going to jail. Right then and there I knew my goose was cooked. As I was sitting nervously in the courtroom, the case just before mine was a drug case. It was this young Spanish gentleman who was being charged with possession of crack cocaine. The judge suspended all jail time and gave him a one-year probation. I said to myself that this guy really got off very lightly for such a charge of that magnitude.

Then it was my turn and I was not feeling any worry considering the last case. After it was all said and done, that judge sentenced me to twelve months in jail with five months suspended. I just stood there with my mouth hung wide open. Not only was I surprised but the officer that put the handcuffs on me and escorted me to the jail was also surprised.

As I sat in the holding area to be processed, I was one unhappy sinner. I mean I really was. All kinds of thoughts were going through my mind such as how am I going to pay rent, phone and electronic bills. How is my landlord going to take me being in jail for this amount of time? What is going to happen with my job and also the rental car that was currently parked in the courthouse parking lot? Then, I said to myself God has a purpose for my life. The living Lord of host has a plan for me in this jail and I know he is not going to let anything happen to me; moreover, he will see to it that all of my bills be paid.

As I waited to be processed the Lord laid on my heart what he wanted me to do. First, get in contact with my lady friend Shorty. That was truly a task because in jail you can only make collect calls and Shorty only has a cell phone and you cannot make collect calls to cell phones. So, what I did was to call someone I knew at their house and gave them my lady friend's cell phone number and asked them to have her come up to the jail so I could give her some very important information.

Everything worked out like clock work. Shorty came up to the jail the next day, and I was allowed to give her my keys so she could drive the car to the house. I also gave her my bank card so she could pay my rent and other bills. I did inform her that I had money direct deposited into my account every third of each month. She understood and did everything I had asked of her. She informed me that she will be staying at my house until I was released from jail. I told her to be my guest because she was doing me a huge favor and that I was truly grateful for her kindness. There was the ordeal of informing my landlord of my situation and after a few days had past, I finally mustard up the nerve to call them. To my surprise they were very understanding of the situation and were also surprised of the judge's decision. I also informed them what Shorty was going to do for me. After that they just wished me well and to hang in there because things would get better for me as if God was speaking to me through them.

From that point I did not have a worry in the world; and moreover, I knew for sure that it was God's will for me to be there in that jail. Here I was in the Fairfax County Adult Detention Center and I tell you this jail was nothing like the Alexandria jail. The Alexandria jail was much newer and the one at Fairfax was very old. Some of the officers treat you like you are the scum of the earth which I thought was a good thing because you could use their behavior toward you as an encouragement to never ever do anything else to come back to jail, PERIOD.

The food they fed you was not prepared properly. However, at least they did feed you. That is the way I looked at it because I totally knew where I was at and could not and would not adjust to the ways of the jail. There were fights almost every day; guys getting seriously hurt for food, fighting for TV rights, and card games. It was truly an adventure being in that jail. I will surely never ever forget it. After a few days I called my job to inform them of my situation and they promptly informed me that they would not be able to hold my job for me. I told them that I truly understood and I also thanked them for allowing me to work for them and that I enjoyed working with them all. They wished me well in this situation I was in.

CHAPTER FORTY EIGHT

The dorms were very small in which I stayed for about two weeks before I was transferred to the work release program. The new dorms had four rooms – two beds in each room and no toilet in the rooms like it is in most jails. The toilet was located right next to the two showers and they had one picnic bench made out of pure solid cement. You talk about being uncomfortable; it truly was and that is a fact. There was one thirteen inch color television hanging over the cement picnic bench,

This is what my day consisted of: you must be out of your room by 6:00 am; and at 7:00 am two officers came into the dorm and locked your room door until 7:00 pm. That is right my beloveds you were not allowed back into your room until 7:00 pm. During that time you would be on that hard floor or concrete hard bench looking at TV. By being on the floor or that hard bench, everyone was sure to have their blanket with them which really did not help very much. Lunch was served at 11:30 am and along with lunch everyone had the opportunity to fill out request forms for whatever need they had. I promptly filled out a form to be transferred to the work release program. My request was granted in two weeks which brought great joy to my heart. Dinner was served at 5:30 pm. An officer would come in and open your cell room door at 7:00 pm. At 11:00 pm the television goes off and back into your cell and if you needed to use the toilet during the night or early morning hours there was a buzzer you pushed to notify the officer. One night I personally pushed that buzzer for twenty five minutes. If I was dying or had a serious emergency, I would have been in serious trouble that night. However, when the officer finally did come I did not say one thing to him but thank you. I did not want to give any of the officers any excuse to do anything to me whatsoever.

During the seven months I was at that jail, I noticed officers trying to make trouble for a lot of the inmates by just literally pushing their buttons and a lot of them succeeded and off they went to the hole. The hole was solitary confinement in which you are put in a very small room all by yourself with no one to talk to and no TV. If you said anything out of the way to the officers, they would not feed you but once a day and on top of that a few of the officers would go in that small hole and beat you senseless. That is what I was told by another inmate.

While lying in my bunk at night I was wondering what God had in store for me in that jail or was I just there for punishment for my evil deeds or maybe both. At the time I really did not know. I was thinking to myself that God does chasten those he loves and then on the other hand maybe it was both; that he does in fact have some work for me to do. Then it struck me like a bolt of lightening. God wants me to work on me and that work is getting my heart right with him. I had a heart problem that was destroying my life.

CHAPTER FORTY NINE

Yes, my dear brothers and sisters God had revealed to me that I had a heart problem from a spiritual standpoint. The word of God suddenly started flowing through my mind concerning my heart condition. As it is written in Jeremiah Chapter 17, verse 9: The heart is deceitful above all things and desperately wicked: who can know it? As I thought on that verse, it was telling me that there is no depth of evil that I am not capable of doing and that very reason is why it was so easy to do the things I was doing before and after receiving Christ Jesus into my life.

As it is written in Matthew Chapter 15, verses 8 and 18-20: This people draweth nigh unto me with their mouth, and honoureth me with their lips; but their heart is far from me. But those things which proceed out of the mouth come forth from the heart; and they defile the man. For out of the heart proceed evil thoughts, murders, adulteries, fornications, thefts, false witness, blasphemies: These are the things which defile a man: But to eat with unwashed hands defileth not a man.

As I thought on these verses, I was only serving God with lip service and that is why I was falling deeper into sin as the days went on when I was using crack and engaged in sexual sin. As it is also written in Luke Chapter 6, verse 45: a good man out of the treasure of his heart bringeth forth that which is good; and an evil man out of the evil treasure of his heart bringeth forth that which is evil: for of the abundance of the heart his mouth speaketh.

I realized that I was only acting on the content of my heart which was nothing but pure evil and that my beloveds was and is a very hurtful feeling especially knowing all that God has truly done and is doing for me. From that point on I knew I needed some serious surgery done on my heart, and I knew the only cure would be the powerful word of God with the guidance of the Holy Spirit and speaking of the Holy Spirit. While I was killing myself with crack cocaine and indulging in immoral sexual sins, I was hindering the performance and the guidance of the Holy Spirit. I was literally stumping my own spiritual growth. As it is written in 1 Thessalonians Chapter 5, verse 19: Quench not the spirit. Also, it is written in Ephesians Chapter 4, verse 30: And grieve not the Holy Spirit of God, whereby ye are sealed unto the day of redemption.

So there you have it my beloveds. It is extremely important for me to watch what I put before my eyes, what I say out of my mouth and basically be very mindful of how I conduct myself so I will not hinder the work of the Holy Spirit in this Life God has so freely given me.

As the nights went on I was also thinking about my kids and how can I be a better parent. At times the flesh was saying to me that I have been nothing but a huge disappointment to myself, my kids and to God Himself. Then, I thought to myself that the devil is trying to make me have a very low self-esteem of myself and doubt that God could and would transform me permanently. The devil was constantly bringing doubt in my mind.

CHAPTER FIFTY

The day had finally arrived for me to be transferred to the work release program. The officers came to my dorm at 12:00 am to take me to the other unit. When I arrived at the unit everyone was asleep and as I looked around it was totally different from the place I had just left. The unit was absolutely huge. It was two levels with about 30 rooms on each level and had two beds in each room. The unit also had two office rooms for the deputies, a fifty inch color TV in the middle of the unit, nine big sofas lined up in rows of three facing the TV, a ping pong table, an ironing board with an iron, and about eight medium sized card tables with four chairs around each table. My brothers and sisters I would say that this unit was a tremendous change from the dorm I just left.

My roommate was a very quiet individual and appeared to be very nice and believe you me that was very comforting and on top of that he did not snore. That was a blessing all in itself. He informed me about the behavior of some of the deputies and the rules and regulations of the program. As I was getting settled in my room that night or very early morning, he also informed me of the hours the unit eats breakfast, lunch and dinner which was 5:30 am breakfast;

11:30 am lunch and dinner was at 6:00 pm. The meals were served in a huge cafeteria where the jail had the women inmates serve the food. It was nice to see women sometimes rather than just men all day.

Back in the other dorm your meals were brought to the dorms and you were not allowed outside the dorm at all unless you were scheduled to see the nurse, the doctor or unless you had a court date. That following morning I had a meeting with one of the directors of the work release program. The program allows an inmate to go out to work and come straight back to the jail from work when he gets paid. The inmate must bring the check straight back to the jail and give it to the accounting department. The accounting department takes the jail's cut off the top (meaning the inmate is charged to be in the program). I believe the charge was 35% of the gross pay and the rest goes into an account for the inmate. When the inmate wants or needs some money for transportation or whatever, the inmate must complete a request form and put it in the inbox of the accounting department which was located next door to the cafeteria.

When each inmate came back from work or looking for work, he was ordered to give a breathalyzer test, If it was positive, he was sent directly back to one of those awful dorms.

Moreover, each inmate was ordered to give periodic urine tests and if it came back positive, off to the hole you go. During my meeting with one of the program directors who was a white lady, she started talking to me in a very nasty way. I mean she talked to me like I stole something from her. I really could not understand why she was doing this because I was not used to being talked to in this fashion. I said under my breath what is this lady's problem. She yelled and said what did you say? I said nothing. She abruptly told me to get out and go back to the unit. At that time I really did not know what to make of what had just happened to me. I went back to the unit to ponder on what had happened for I was truly confused. I informed some of the guys what had happened and they asked me who I was talking to. I told them and they said that she is normally very nice. Well, I said to them that something is dreadfully wrong with her this day and that was a fact because I did not do anything to cause her to talk to me the way she did.

Later that evening at almost 8:00 pm one of the deputies came to the unit and told me to pack my bags because I was being transferred to the park services unit which was located right below the work release program. While I was packing my bags, my roommate asked me what happened, so I told him. He informed me that where I was going was not bad at all and that the park service unit looked just like the work release unit.

After packing all of my belongings, I said my good-byes to the few inmates I had met. As the deputy was taking me downstairs he informed me that I would be in the park service unit for 30 days. Then I would be sent back to the work release program. My brothers and sisters those 30 days turned into 60 days; however, I did not complain. Now when that deputy opened the door to the park service unit, the very first thing I noticed to my surprise and also to my delight, was about five inmates were gathered around a table having bible study.

CHAPTER FIFTY ONE

When I saw those inmates gathered at that table having bible study, a feeling went through me that I really could not explain at that moment. However, later I would say that it was a feeling of relief as truly knowing what purpose God had for me being in that jail. My beloveds the next two months would be a life changing experience I would not trade for anything in this world.

After I settled in my room, I promptly went to that table and introduced myself to the five guys and asked them if I could join in. They said, yes of course. Even though it was at the tail end of the meeting, I arrived in time to join them in prayer. After praying one of the guys who appeared to be the leader introduced himself to me as well as the other guys.

The guy who appeared to be the leader, I will just call him 'leader' throughout the rest of this book, went on to tell me that the bible study meeting was every night at 7:00 pm and each guy takes a turn in leading the meeting, coming up with any topic of their choosing. I knew I was going to love this.

From there he went on to inform me about the park service program itself. It is a program where they have everyone go down to the cafeteria at 9:00 am where they have four deputies who literally run the program. They choose seven to ten inmates to go out and work, doing such things as pulling trash from bus stops all over Fairfax and Alexandria, cutting grass, painting and/or cleaning.

Throughout the two months I was in that unit I was never picked to go out; however, it did not bother me at all because it gave me a chance to really focus on the task I had at hand. So, the only thing I did was study the word of God and play ping pong, a game that I used to play a lot of when I was younger. When I first started I was a little rusty; however, I became a lot better as the days rolled on.

Breakfast was at 6:00 am, lunch at 12:00 pm and dinner at 5:30 pm. The unit was in fact designed the same way as the work release unit. My roommate was a quiet fellow just like the one I had before. The only difference with this roommate is that he was a very good ping pong player. After coming to this unit I knew that it was God's will for me to be there and everything happened in accordance of his plan for this life God has so freely given me. So, as the days went on it seemed as if the word of God was coming alive within me with great power. I remember when the guys called on me to close out the meeting with prayer for the first time. When I finished the guys just stared at me as well as the other inmates that were playing cards and the other inmates that were looking at the TV. They were looking at me with amazement. The guys at the table said it was a very moving prayer. As the time continued I really looked forward to my first time to lead the bible study meeting. I was very happy with what God was doing in this unit. It has been a long time since my heart felt this much joy.

CHAPTER FIFTY TWO

The time had finally come around for me to lead the bible study and my topic was bible basics. The Lord laid upon my heart that topic because it is very important for every believer to at least know the basics before going on to the meat of the word if you will. As it is written in 1 Peter Chapter 2, verse 2: As newborn babes, desire the sincere milk of the word that ye may grow thereby.

Now I will share with you my first bible study that I shared with my fellow inmates. I will be sharing with you the contents of this study which will involve sixteen questions along with the answers from the living word of God that relate to bible basic information that all believers in Christ should in fact know.

Bible Basics

1. What does the word bible mean? Book of Books.
2. How many books are there in the bible? 66: 39 in the Old Testament and 27 in the new.

3. How did the world begin? Genesis Chapter 1 – in the beginning God created the heaven and the earth.

4. Where did man come from? Genesis Chapter 2, verse 7: And the Lord God formed man of the dust of the ground, and breathed into his nostrils the breath of life; and man became a living soul.

5. For what purpose was man created? Isaiah Chapter 43, verse 7: Even every one that is called by my name: for I have created him for my glory, I have formed him; yea, I have made him. And, Colossians Chapter 1, verses 13-16: Who hath delivered us from the power of darkness, and has translated us into the kingdom of his dear son: In whom we have redemption through his blood, even the forgiveness of sins: who is the image of the invisible God, the firstborn of every creature: For by him were all things created, that are in heaven, and that are in earth, visible and invisible, where they be thrones, or dominions, or principalities, or powers: all things were created by him and for him.

6. How did sin enter into the world? Genesis Chapter 3: Now the serpent was more subtle than any beast of the field which the Lord God had made, and he said unto the woman, yea, hath God said, ye shall not eat of every tree of the garden? And the woman said unto the serpent, we may eat of the fruit of the trees of the garden: But of the fruit of the tree which is in the midst of the garden, God hath said, ye shall not eat of it, neither shall ye touch it, lest ye die. And the serpent said unto the woman, ye shall not surely die: For God doth know that in the day ye eat thereof, then your eyes shall be opened, and ye shall be as gods, knowing good and evil. And when the woman saw that the tree was good for food, and that it was pleasant to the eyes, and a tree to be desired to make one wise, she took of the fruit thereof, and did eat, and gave also unto her husband with her; and he did eat it.

7. What are the 10 commandments? Exodus Chapter 20:

1. Thou shalt have no other gods before me.

2. Thou shalt not make unto thee any graven image, or any likeness of any thing that is in heaven above, or that is in the earth beneath, or that is in the water under the earth. Thou shalt not bow down thyself to them, nor serve them: for I the Lord thy God am a

jealous God, visiting the iniquity of the fathers upon the children unto the third and fourth generation of them that hate me; and shewing mercy unto thousands of them that love me, and keep my commandments.

3. Thou shalt not take the name of the Lord thy God in vain; for the Lord will not hold him guiltless that taketh his name in vain.

4. Remember the Sabbath day and keep it holy. Six days shalt thou labor and do all thy work: but the seventh day is the Sabbath of the Lord thy God: in it thou shalt not do any work, thou, nor thy son, nor thy daughter, thy manservant, nor thy maidservant, nor thy cattle, nor thy stranger that is within thy gates: for in six days the Lord made heaven and earth, the sea, and all that in them is, and rested the seventh day: wherefore the Lord blessed the Sabbath day, and hollowed it.

5. Honour thy father and thy mother: that thy days may be long upon the land which the Lord thy God giveth thee.

6. Thou shalt not kill.

7. Thou shalt not commit adultery.

8. Thou shalt not bear false witness against thy neighbor.

9. Thou shalt not steal.

10. Thou shalt not covet thy neighbor's house, thou shalt not covet thy neighbor's wife, nor his manservant, nor his maidservant, nor his ox, nor his ass, nor any thing that is thy neighbors.

8. Is everybody a sinner? Romans Chapter 3, verse 23: For all have sinned, and come short of the glory of God.

9. What is sin? Romans Chapter 3, verse 20: Therefore, by the deeds of the law there shall no flesh be justified in his sight: for by the law is the knowledge of sin.

10. What are the two classes of people upon this earth: 1 John Chapter 5, verses 11-12: And this is the record that God hath given to us eternal life and this life is in his Son. He that hath the Son hath life; and he that hath not the Son of God hath not life.

11. What is the outcome of living a life without Christ Jesus? Revelations Chapter 21, verse 8: But the fearful, and the unbelieving, and the abominable, and murderers, and whoremongers, and sorcerers, and idolaters, and all liars, shall have their part in the

lake of which burneth with fire and brimstone: which is the second death.

Luke Chapter 16, verses 19-25: There was a certain rich man, which was clothed in purple and fine linen, and fared sumptuously every day: and there was a certain begger named Lazarus, which was laid at his gate, full of sores, and desiring to be fed with the crumbs which fell from the rich man's table: moreover, the dogs came and licked his sores. And it came to pass, that the begger died, and was carried by the angels into Abraham's bosom: The rich man also died, and was buried; and in hell he lifted up his eyes, being in torments, and seeing Abraham afar off and Lazarus in his bosom. And he cried and said, father Abraham, have mercy on me, and send Lazarus that he may dip the tip of his finger in water, and cool my tongue; for I am tormented in this flame. But Abraham said, son, remember that thou in thy lifetime receivedst thy good things, and likewise Lazarus evil things: But now he is comforted, and thou art tormented.

12. What is the outcome of living a life with Christ Jesus? Matthew Chapter 11, verses 28-30: Come unto me, all ye that labour and are heavy laden, and I will give you rest. Take my yoke upon you, and learn of me; for I am meek and lowly in heart: and ye shall find rest unto your souls. For my yoke is easy, and my burden is light.

St. John Chapter 10, verse 10: The thief cometh not, but for to steal, and to kill, and to destroy: I am come that they might have life, and that they might have more abundantly.

Philippians Chapter 4, verse 19: But my God shall supply all your need according to his riches in glory by Christ Jesus.

Matthew Chapter 6, verse 33: But seek ye first the Kingdom of God, and his righteousness; and all these things shall be added unto you.

13. How does mankind obtain salvation? Romans Chapter 10, verses 9-10: That if thou shalt confess with thy mouth the Lord Jesus, and believe in thine heart that God hath raised him from the dead, thou shalt be saved. For with the heart man believeth unto righteousness; and with the mouth confession is made unto salvation.

1 Timothy Chapter 4, verse 10: For therefore we both labour and suffer reproach, because we trust in the living God, who is the saviour of all men, especially of those that believe.

St. John Chapter 3, verse 36: He that believeth on the Son hath life: and he that believeth not the Son shall not see life; but the wrath of God abideth on him.

14. How do we fight against sin and the devil? Ephesians Chapter 6, verses 10-20: Finally, my brethren, be strong in the Lord, and in the power of his might. Put on the whole armour of God that ye may be able to stand against the wiles of the devil. For we wrestle not against flesh and blood, but the rulers of the darkness of this world, against spiritual wickedness in high places. Wherefore, take unto you the whole armour of God that ye may be able to withstand in the evil day, and having done all, to stand. Stand therefore, having your loins girt about with truth, and having the breastplate of righteousness; and your feet shod with the preparation of the gospel of peace; above all, taking the shield of faith, wherewith ye shall be able to quench all the fiery darts of the wicked. And take the helmet of salvation, and the sword of the spirit, which is the word of God: praying always with all prayer and supplication in the spirit, and watching thereunto with all perseverance and supplication for all saints; and for me that utterance may be given unto me, that I may open my mouth boldly, to make known the mystery of the gospel, for which I am an ambassador in bonds: that therein I may speak boldly, as I ought to speak.

15. Who wrote the bible? 2 Timothy Chapter 3, verse 16: All scripture is given by inspiration of God, and is profitable for doctrine, for reproof, for correction, for instruction in righteousness.

16. What is the purpose of the bible? 2 Timothy Chapter 3, verses 16-17: All scripture is given by inspiration of God, and is profitable for doctrine, for reproof, for correction, for instruction in righteousness; that the man of God may be perfect (meaning complete), thoroughly (meaning completely), furnished unto all good works.

I must say after that study, things were beginning to change in that unit. I mean the word of God was taking a serious hold on many of the inmate's hearts, not to mention especially my own heart. When I first came into that unit, the bible study group number was just six including myself and after just a few weeks it had ballooned up to about twelve. During the time I was in that unit, I was seeing deputies listening in on the studies, inmates being saved and basically many of the inmates having a new outlook on life itself. After the 30 days were up, I found myself still in that unit. I was given the opportunity to speak with the deputy that was the head of the work release program. He informed me that it would be very soon and he also said next time you will learn to keep your mouth shut. I said to him, yes, you are right and thank you, knowing in my heart that I did nothing to provoke that lady's actions. As the days continued to pass, there was a click in the unit that displayed a rough and tough attitude. A click is what you would call a small group of guys that hang with each other all the time. The leader of the bible study group came to my room while I was preparing my studies for the night's meeting and informed me that a couple of the guys from the click were going to attend the group and try to trip me up or find holes in what I was going to teach. He said that he overheard them talking and went on to say do not be nervous and to do a good job. I promptly told him that it was not going to be me but the Holy Spirit busy at work. That night the topic was on prayer and the importance of prayer. Right after I opened the meeting with prayer, the ring leader of the click opened up his mouth by saying, 'How can you ask God for this and that without saying that you are sorry for the things you have done wrong?' My reply was that when I prayed I personally started off with the Lord's Prayer. He, the ring leader of the click, cut me off and started getting loud saying that what I said did not make any sense at all and that I needed to shut up. I saw right through him and saw what he was trying to do; however, I did not let it phase me because I knew the Lord was in full control. Now after he had finished ranting and raving, I asked him (with my voice that was filled with great peace), could I continue? He angrily said go right ahead. I explained to him and the group the Lord's Prayer line by line and especially the verse that states, forgive us our debts, as we forgive our debtors (Matthew Chapter 6, verse 12). After that I went on to give the group my prayer outline as written earlier in this book. After the study I closed in prayer and when I started to pray a great hush came over the entire unit. Someone had even turned down the TV. It was an awesome experience to behold. I mean it really was. After that study the leader of the click walked over to me and said, 'great job – that was alright'. My response to him was, God is a good God and is all powerful. He and his click just went on their merry way and for the next few nights just hung out right over the railings to listen in on the meetings. However, they never came back to join us at the table. Unfortunately for the click, the following week every last one of them was put out of the unit because of being caught smoking cigarettes in the bathroom. I would say the Lord dealt swiftly with them and mightily without question. I would also say that the Lord hates those that have a seriously evil heart. One day as I was coming from lunch I saw that the head deputy of the work release program. He informed me to get ready because I was going back up to the work release program in a couple of days. After receiving the news, I knew I had one more study that I had to lead and I wanted it to be a very powerful message that would sink deep into our hearts. God gave me the grace and strength to come up with a commentary on love. I felt the commentary that the Lord gave me to write was really powerful and would truly fill our hearts with hope.

CHAPTER FIFTY THREE

The Love Commentary

There is a song that states love means never having to say you are sorry. Webster says love means warm affection, sexual passion. The meanings or definitions that I just shared with you may relate; however, it is not the kind of love that will be talked about or discussed this day. In order for us being Christians to live a victorious life upon this evil world we live in, it is very important for us to know the true love of God, to know how to obtain the love of God in our hearts, to share the love of God with everyone we come in contact with. And last, is to allow the love of God to truly rule the very life God has so freely given us all.

As being the sinners we are, we must understand that we are separated from God's love from the beginning of our existence. As it is written in Romans Chapter 5, verse 12: Wherefore, as by one man sin entered into the world, and death by sin; and so death passed upon all men, for that all have sinned. Psalms Chapter 51, verse 5: Behold, I was shapen in iniquity, and in sin did my mother conceive me.

So it is impossible for us to have God's love living in our hearts before committing to the living Lord Jesus Christ. We must all ask ourselves first, am I totally if at all committed or surrendered to Jesus Christ; can I say my life reflects the character of Jesus Christ; is my language free from wickedness, vile, and evil words; and do I find myself sharing unconditional love with everyone I come in contact with?

It is very important to ask ourselves this question. Can I say without a shadow of a doubt that I love the Lord with all of my heart, mind, body and soul? If not, it is time that we all examine our hearts and lives thoroughly, perform if you will an inventory of the life we have been living. Then, allow God to take full control of this life God has so free given us all. Then and only then will be able to live a victorious life that God would have for us to live.

In order for us to obtain this unconditional love, we must first realize our lost condition without Christ Jesus. As it is written in John Chapter 3, verse 36: He that believeth on the Son hath everlasting life; and he that believeth not the Son shall not see life; but the wrath of God (abideth) which means (will stay) on him.

Humbly ask Jesus Christ to be the Lord of our life. As it is written in Romans Chapter 10, verses 9-10: If thou shalt confess with they mouth the Lord Jesus, and shalt believe in thine heart that God hath raised him from the dead, thou shalt be saved, for with the heart man believeth unto righteousness; and with the mouth confession is made into salvation.

Feed on God's holy word every day. As it is written in 1 Peter Chapter 2, verse 2: As new born babes, desire the sincere milk of the word that ye may grow thereby.

Develop a prayer life. As it is written in James Chapter, verse 16: Confess your faults one to another, and pray one for another, that ye may be healed. The effectual (which means unceasing) fervent prayer of a righteous man availeth much.

As we do what I have mentioned, the love of God will begin to grow in our hearts with great power through the Holy Spirit.

In closing, the way to know if the love of God is operating in our lives, ask yourself if 1st John Chapter 4, verses 20-21 states: If a man say, I love God, and hateth his brother, he is a liar: for he that loveth not his brother whom he hath seen, how can he love God whom he hath not seen? And this commandment have we from him, that he who loveth God love his brother also, is operating in our hearts on a daily basis.

After reading this commentary, I strongly suggest that you read all of Chapter 13 (called the love chapter) in 1 Corinthians and be studied very carefully for your admonition. As it is written: Though I speak with the tongues of men and of angels, and have not charity (which means love), I am become as sounding brass, or a tinkling cymbal. And though I have the gift of prophecy, and understand all mysteries, and all knowledge; and though I have all faith, so that I could remove mountains, and have not charity, I am nothing. And though I bestow all goods to feed the poor, and though I give my body to be burned, and have not charity, it profiteth me nothing.

Charity suffereth long, and is kind; charity envieth not; charity vaunteth not itself, is not puffed up, doth not behave itself unseemly, seeketh not her own, is not easily provoked, thinketh no evil; rejoiceth not in iniquity, but rejoiceth in truth; beareth all things, believeth all things, hopeth all things, endureth all things.

Charity never faileth: but whether there be prophecies, they shall fail; whether there be tongues, they shall cease; whether there be knowledge, it shall vanquish away. For we know in part, and we prophesy in part. But when that which is perfect is come, then that which is in part shall be done away.

When I was a child, I spake as a child, I understood as a child, I thought as a child: but when I became a man, I put away childish things. For now we see through a glass, darkly; but then face to face: now I know in part; but then shall I know even as also I am known. And now abideth faith, hope, charity, these three; but the greatest of these is charity. May God open the hearts and minds to the readers and hearers of this commentary and give understanding in their hearts through the power of the Holy Spirit. AMEN

As I finished reading this commentary everyone that was gathered at the bible study was truly moved – myself included. The spirit of the Lord was truly at work in that unit. After the end of the study, all of the guys wanted a copy of the commentary. So, the next day I asked one of the ladies that worked in the accounting department if she would make the copies for me. After she did, she informed me that she made a copy for herself. I must say that it really moved me when she said that. It was really an encouragement to me to press on that I might continue to bring much glory to the Lord of all – none other than the living Lord Jesus Christ.

The time had come for me to move back to the work release program. The Lord used jail to help me to see my purpose in life. The guys and I exchanged phone numbers and said our goodbyes and said a small prayer just before I left the unit. I will never forget what God did in that unit.

Chapter Fifty Four

When I arrived back at the work release program at about 7:30 pm, I saw a few of the guys that were in the park service unit I had just left. When one of the guys saw me, he came over and promptly informed me in a joking fashion that there is no bible study going on up here. My response was, 'Well, we just have to see what the Lord has to say about that'. He promptly left with a grimacing look on his face.

As I settled in my room, I was truly unhappy being put in a room where the air conditioning was not working. The guy that was in the room already did not seem to care. The very next day I filled out a request form to please be moved. They moved me but not before two weeks had past. It was mid summer and I am in a room where the air conditioner is not working. I thought to myself that I could be back in the dorm where I was originally placed when I first went to jail. I must say that dorm is a true incentive for me personally to not EVER do anything that would cause me to be locked up and I mean that from the bottom of my heart my beloveds.

The following morning came, my first day back in the work release program. I thought to myself that I was given the opportunity to meet with the same lady as before and to my surprise she was completely different. I mean she treated me very kindly and I really did not know what to make of it. I thought to myself she may have heard about the bible studies that took place while I was at the other unit; I just did not know. More than likely it was God's will for me to be in that park service unit first, because he had work for me to do there. In any event, I know that God used me in a mighty way, and I am quite sure he is going to do the same thing in the unit I was now in.

The meeting with the lady who is one of the coordinators of the program informed me of the rules and regulations and had me to fill out some paperwork. Just before you go out to look for work, they give you a list of jobs. Then you have to write down where you are going and how much time you will need. I had a job within one week at the NTB (National Tire and Battery) which was very close to the jail. My job consisted of changing tires, oil changes and fixing flats. My brothers and sisters I really hated that job because it was hard work. It was summer time which means it was very hot in the work area and the manager was not very nice. He felt that he could treat you any way he wanted because we were from the jail. There were several guys already there from the jail, five including myself. However, I humbled myself because I only had until December, five months to go.

After being back in the unit for a couple of days I asked the Lord to send someone my way to help me to get a bible study group started. In one day the Lord sent two. I mean I was sitting at one of the tables going through my bible and behold two inmates showed up with bibles in their hands ready to dig into the living word of God., After witnessing what I just shared with you, I will never ever doubt the power of the living and true God. The living Lord has truly revealed himself to me in that jail.

CHAPTER FIFTY FIVE

A bible study had now officially been started in the work release program. It was somewhat hard at first to nail down a time for bible study on a regular basis because of everyone's work schedule. After about two weeks we being five now finally came up with 8:00 am for the time for us to start our study group. The bible study group adopted the same system that the other group had, such as each person taking turns leading the group by picking a topic of their choosing.

Everything was going so well that one day the vendor came to me to give me a compliment on how I was running the bible study group. He informed me that when he came in the mornings to fill the vending machines, he noticed how I came downstairs to set up for the meetings and also how I led off with prayer and scripture reading. I promptly told him that it is the living true God that leads this group and God is only using me as a vessel to carry out his will or work if you please.

As the days continued on, the group was really growing in numbers to about ten to twelve inmates. And, the beauty of it all was that it was different nationalities from just about all races. It was a beautiful thing to behold.

The Lord had sent a really strong brother in the Lord. I mean this brother really offered strong prayers in the beginning and ending of the meetings. I knew when I left he would make sure the group continued with the work of the Lord. When the month of October rolled around, I was offered a program called the home incarceration program which consisted of wearing an ankle bracelet that you could not remove and also a device the size of a small transistor radio that you would attach to your waist or belt buckle whenever you left your home. You also had to have a home phone in order for the program coordinators to set up the program. The program attaches a transmitter that has a phone line jack that would be connected to your phone line.

For instance if you would leave your home without the small transistor radio, an alarm would sound off at the jail along with the transmitter that is hooked up to your phone. There was also a charger you would place the transistor radio in when you arrived back home. You would have to notify the jail in advance of your work schedule, inform them the time you wanted to go to the grocery store, or notify them of your doctor's appointment.

The program would put these times in your transmitter from the jail and last, you would have to call the jail when you left and returned to your home. This particular program cost $420 a month. Since I had more than enough in my account to cover the cost for three months, I accepted this program. It also came to the point where the bible study group was going very strong. The guys in the group were encouraging me to go for it and last, I felt in my heart that I had finished the work the Lord had for me to do while I was in jail. Basically, I had finished the course God laid out for me, plus I truly missed my kids very much.

CHAPTER FIFTY SIX

Now that I was finally back at home with a bracelet around my ankle, I was somewhat embarrassed to be seen with it. So, I made sure the pants I was wearing covered it up completely and the jacket I wore covered the small transistor radio I had to attach to my waist or belt buckle. As for my lady friend, Shorty, I had her to meet me at the house along with the deputies that escorted me to my house so they could set up the transmitter to my phone.

In the process of the deputies hooking up the devise to my phone, Shorty, gave me back my keys, bank card, and informed me that everything was done as far as my rent and bills were concerned. She also went on to tell me that she had moved into her own place and that she has a new friend.

At first I was a little hurt but in the long run I was relieved of not having the temptation of sexual immorality hanging around in my heart. So really, it was of course a blessing from the Lord. As the days and months passed, I continued to work at the National Tire and Battery shop. Some of the guys I worked with said that the meetings were still going strong which made me feel very good inside. I had asked the manager if I could have some Sundays off so I could go to church. His response to that was, 'I will see what I can do'.

My brother and sisters I never received a Sunday off. I really did not want to go to church with a bracelet around my ankle anyway; however, I was willing to do it because of the love of God that truly dwells in my heart. Moreover, the word of God tells me as it is written in Hebrews Chapter 10, verses 23-25: Let us hold fast the profession of our faith without wavering; (for he is faithful that promised;) and let us consider one another to provoke unto love and to good works: Not forsaking (which means neglecting) the assembling of ourselves together, as the manner of some is; but exhorting (which means encouraging) one another: and so much the more, as ye see the day approaching.

I felt and still feel today that going to church is very vital in my Christian walk because I feel that God commands us Christians to practice true fellowship with one another. During the time I was in the home incarceration program, I was building my relationship with the Lord and my kids. I briefly shared with the pastor of the Ark of Love my situation. He promptly gave me words of encouragement that really touched my heart.

During the time I was in that program, I was ordered to report to the jail every other weekend to give a breathalyzer and a urine sample. There were no problems at all and everything went very well for me.

As I prepared for Christmas, my departure date from the program and the court system was December 24, 2005, the eve we celebrate the birth of God's gift to humanity, the living Lord Jesus Christ. I thought to myself more and more that it was in fact God's will for me to go through what I did as far as being jailed because it did me a lot of good and in the process God used me for his glory.

Chapter Fifty Seven

Now that I was free from the home incarceration program and the court system, I felt truly like a new creation in Christ. Without hesitation I started going back to church, going to my daughter's church and on top of that I found a new job working at the Best Western Hotel as a houseman and later transferred to the front desk as a front desk agent. The hotel was located just five minutes from my house which was a blessing. So, I had no need for a rental car or car period at this time. The only thing I would say I truly needed was to continue to feed on the word of the true and living God, continue to fellowship with my brothers and sisters in Christ, and to be a loving parent to my kids.

As far as what I desired, the only thing at this time was for me to be a loving servant of the living Lord Jesus Christ and to win as many souls to the Lord as I possibly can. That is my main purpose for this book and my main goal in life period. I truly want my life to reflect the love of Jesus Christ with everyone I come in contact with, in other words, I want the light that shines in my heart to be reflected in my behavior. As it is written in Matthew Chapter, verse

16: Let your light so shine before men, that they may see your good works, and glorify your father which is in heaven.

At this time I want to share the last commentary I wrote which was for the Black History church program in 2007.

Black History Commentary 2007

This time of year we come together to acknowledge Black History Month. We acknowledge black men and women who have made an impact on the human race and their struggles in the process. We also acknowledge our race as a whole which has been oppressed with slavery, racism, and many other offenses; however, in spite of all the difficulties our race has been through, by the grace of the true and living God, we managed to endure and to overcome it all; well, almost all.

Briefly, I would like to share with you the slavery our race is going through today. It is pertaining to more of a spiritual nature. As I look at the news, and go out to witness, I experience it first hand how our race is suffering from spiritual blindness. The result of this is bondage and slavery to sin. Yes, I have seen for myself, other men, women and children of our race are being held in bondage to self and the world.

The effects of this bondage is as follows: teenage pregnancies; drug and alcohol addiction; a horrendous amount of one parent homes; suicides; divorces at an alarming rate; hearts filled with much hatred; drive by shootings in black neighborhoods; kids bringing guns to school and killing one another; little young black children in public using vile and evil language that is truly unbecoming even for an adult. That is just to name a few. When I see these things, it reminds me of what is written in the word of God in Romans Chapter 3, verses 10-18: There is none righteous, no not one: There is none that understandeth, there is none that seeketh after God. They are all gone out of the way, they are together become unprofitable (which means useless); their throat is an open sepulcher (which means grave); with their tongues they have used deceit; the poison of asps (which means snakes) is under their lips: whose mouth is full of cursing and bitterness: their feet are swift to shed blood: destruction and misery are in their ways: and the way of peace have they not known: there is no fear of God before their eyes.

That my precious ones is what I see mostly in our race today. Still, there is no fear of God before our eyes. This particular slavery I have mentioned to you today is running rampant in our race with great fury. We as a race and fellow servants in one body (meaning the church); truly need to come together and make a stand against this slavery that is destroying our race.

You may be asking yourselves how we as one body could make a stand against this evil slavery? Let me share with you some of the ways we could make a stand. If you are truly a born again Christian and are in fact allowing the love of Christ Jesus to rule in your hearts and desire to be a soul winner, then pass out tracts (meaning little booklets that have God's plan of salvation printed in it); be a living testimony of God's great love and transforming power, and support your local church fervently. Think of ways your church could have a stronger impact in the community and basically be more giving of yourselves to others as Christ Jesus gave and is giving of himself for us wretched sinners. Please carry these scriptures in your heart for the rest of the days God allows you to be upon this earth.

1. As it is written in Romans Chapter 12, verse 1: Beseech (meaning beg) you therefore brethren, by the mercies of God, that you present (meaning yield) your bodies a living sacrifice, holy acceptable unto God, which is your reasonable service.

2. As it is written in Colossians Chapter 1, verse 16: For by him were all things created, that are in heaven, and earth, visible and invisible, whether they be thrones, or dominions, or principalities, or powers: all things were created by him and for him.

There you have it. We are all to live our lives that God has so freely given us to please him and not our carnal (meaning worldly) nature. If we are truly servants of the living Lord Jesus Christ, we will in fact desire to bring glory to him and make a difference in this thing called life.

Fortunately, by the grace of the true and living God, we have many black men and women who have made a major impact in this thing called life. I could take this time to get into the accomplishments that many black men and women have made; however, instead, I would like to share something with you that should encourage us all and at the very least, give us something to think about.

Since we are talking about black history, I would like to take this time to get somewhat deeper in this subject from a different prospective – a close and personal view from an individual standpoint. I would like for us all that are gathered here today to reflect on the history our own lives have impacted this evil world we live in. Let us ask ourselves, is the life we are living making a positive history or a negative history. Little do we know, our lives are in fact making history. When we fill out an application for a job, there is a section that asks for our job history. Yes, my beloveds, the very life we are living is truly making history.

I feel it is imperative (which means very important, an absolute must) for us to remember that we are in fact making history each day God gives us upon this evil world we live in. Moreover, let us ask ourselves how is the history we are making impacting the hearts of our family members, loved ones, co-workers, friends and most importantly God Himself. After we have passed away from this life, hopefully all of us present will be with the Lord. What will be discussed about the history we left behind?

More important, the history we make will reflect our good and bad works. Let us always keep in our hearts of what it says in the word of God concerning this matter. As it is written in 1 Corinthians, Chapter 3, verses 13-15: Every man's work shall be made manifest (meaning made known): for the day shall declare it, because it shall be revealed by fire; and the fire shall try every man's work of what sort it is.

If a man's work abides which he hath built thereupon, he shall receive a reward. If a man's work shall be burned, he shall suffer lost: but he himself shall be saved; yet so as by fire. Yes, my precious ones, the history we are making is being monitored by God Himself.

In closing my beloveds, I just like to say, let us all make history by leaving an imprint in the hearts of our love one and basically every one we come in contact with, a life history that was Christ filled. I truly thank you all for allowing me to share this black history commentary with you. May God use this commentary to draw us closer unto Him. Again, thank you very much and may God so richly bless you all, AMEN.

When it was time for me to share this commentary, it snowed that weekend and most church services were cancelled. Lord willing it will be shared in the next upcoming Black History Program for 2008.

At this stage of my life that God has blessed me with, I am allowing God's love to live through me, winning souls to Christ by sharing God's word to as many as I possibly can. For it is written in Romans Chapter 10, verses 14-15: How then shall they call on him in whom they have not believed? And how shall they believe in him of whom they have not heard? And how shall they hear without a preacher? And how shall they preach, except they be sent? As it is written, how beautiful are the feet of them that preach the gospel of peace, and bring glad tidings of good things!

Well my beloveds, I truly hope with all of my heart that many around the world read this book and that many souls be saved and many hearts be transformed for the purpose of God alone. May this book be used to bring glory to the God of all, AMEN.

In closing, I truly want to share with the readers how I model my life and that is by Romans 12 which I feel should be read every day.

Chapter Fifty Eight

Personally, I call Romans Chapter 12, the Christian conduct blueprint on how to live our life that God has so freely given us all. As it is written in Romans Chapter 12: I beseech (which means beg) you therefore, brethren, by the mercies of God, that ye present your bodies a living sacrifice, holy, acceptable unto God, which is your reasonable service. And be not conformed to this world: but be ye transformed by the renewing of your mind, that ye may prove what is that good, and acceptable, and perfect, will of God. For I say, through the grace given unto me, to every man that is among you, not to think of himself more highly than he ought to think; but to think soberly (meaning to be of sound mind), according as God hath dealt to every man the measure of faith. For as we have many members in one body, and all members have not the same office: So we, being many, are one body in Christ, and every one members one of another. Having then gifts differing according to the grace that is given to us, whether prophecy, let us prophesy according to the proportion of faith; or ministry, let us wait on our ministering: or he that teacheth, on teaching; or he that exhorteth (which means encourage), on exhortation: he that giveth, let him do it with simplicity; he that ruleth, with diligence; he that sheweth mercy, with cheerfulness. Let love be without dissimulation. Abhor that which is evil; cleave to that which is good. Be kindly affectioned one to another with brotherly love; in honour preferring one another; not slothful in business; fervent in spirit; serving the Lord; rejoicing in hope; patient in tribulation; continuing instant in prayer; distributing to the necessity of saints; given to hospitality. Bless them which persecute you: bless, and curse not. Rejoice with them that do rejoice, and weep with them that weep. Be of the same mind one toward another, mind not high things, but condescend to men of low estate. Be not wise in your own conceit. Recompense to no man evil for evil. Provide things honest in the sight of all men. If it is possible as much as liveth in you, live peaceably with all men. Dearly beloved, avenge not yourselves, but rather give place unto wrath: for it is written – Vengeance is mine; I will repay, saith the Lord. Be not overcome of evil, but overcome evil with good.

There you have it my beloveds. If we all follow the guidelines laid down to us from Romans 12, we will be able to enjoy the life that God has truly blessed us with, and in so doing make this a much better world to live in – especially for our kids. May God bless us all bountifully, AMEN.

CHAPTER FIFTY NINE

The year is now 2010: My life that God has so freely give me has taken on a mirage of changes; however, all good changes mind you. My relationship with the Lord is stronger than ever. My relationship with my children is stronger than I could have ever imagined. My daughter is going on missionary trips with her church to places such as Ghana, Holy Land (Jerusalem), etc. My daughter continues to be a strong influence in my life. My son is preparing to join the Army. My son and I have built a very strong bond with each other. By the loving grace of God, I am still drug free and have no desire to going back to that evil lifestyle – praise the Lord of Host.

I now work at the Holiday Inn Hotel rather than at the Best Western. I started working there in September 2007. I enjoy the family oriented atmosphere at the hotel which brings joy to my heart. In 2007 I purchased a 2007 Ford Taurus. The Lord continues to shower me with many blessings. The only downside to my story is that the Ark of Love Baptist Church has closed its doors for the last time in 2009 due to lack of money because the congregation was very small. However, the pastor and I continue to keep in contact with one another, and he is still a father figure in my life – that God has blessed me with. I also truly miss the assistant chaplin of the Salvation Army that has passed on to be with the Lord. God had used him to lead me into the family of Christ Jesus.

I am praying that the Lord will use me to lead many into the body (meaning church) of Jesus Christ. I am now attending the Woodlawn Baptist Church and am now building a relationship with the pastor there. I am currently not in a serious relationship with a female. I am presently focusing on building an even stronger relationship with my Lord and Savior Jesus Christ.

I have learned that life will bring many difficult situations my way. However, when I am truly trusting in the Lord for guidance and direction, everything will work out perfectly. (As it is written: In God's word in Romans Chapter 8: all things work for good for those who love God and that are called according to his purpose, Amen).

Life can be a beautiful thing when the Lord Jesus Christ is in the center of it all, my dear brothers and sisters. May the Lord Jesus Christ bless everyone who reads this book.

The End

Printed in the United States
By Bookmasters